The
Teacher of the Year
HaNDBOOK

The Ultimate Guide to Making the Most of
Your Teacher-Leader Role

BY **Alex Kajitani,**
CALIFORNIA TEACHER OF THE YEAR

WITH Megan Pincus Kajitani

• SECOND EDITION •

The authors would like to dedicate this book to their parents, who taught them both to be teachers and leaders.

A Kajitani Education publication — *Educating for the world as it can be.*

Cover & Layout Design by Bamboo Star Studios
Author Photograph by Earnie Grafton, *San Diego Union-Tribune*

TABLE OF CONTENTS

"We are all concerned about the future of American education. But as I tell my students, you do not enter the future — you create the future."

- Jaime Escalante

CHAPTER 1

INTRODUCTION:
WHAT TO EXPECT WHEN YOU'RE SELECTED

AND THE TEACHER OF THE YEAR IS...

There I was, sitting with my pregnant wife, in a beautiful old theater in downtown San Diego, dressed in a fancy suit among a packed crowd, watching videos of San Diego County's amazing District Teachers of the Year on the screens above the stage. So many emotions swirled through my mind...

Gratitude *that our county actually honors teachers with a show like this, and that I was among the teachers in this audience.*

Desire *to be chosen as a County Teacher of the Year, mostly because I had "big ideas" about education that I wanted to share, and bigger work I wanted to do.*

Fear *for my family — which also included our toddler left all evening with a sitter for the first time, ready to blow at any moment — because I had chosen to be a teacher, and I wanted to be able to support them, while doing this work I am passionate about.*

Doubt *that I was really doing anything worth recognizing more than any other of the thousands of teachers out there, giving their all each day for students, the same as I was.*

Hope *that perhaps I was sitting there in that theater because it was time for me to step up, as an educator, and as a man, and make a bigger impact in the world.*

1

As the night ticked on, finalists were chosen from each group of teachers featured on the videos. I had not been featured yet. I began to sweat and shift in my seat as the final group of teachers appeared on the screen. This was it, make it or break it.

My wife squeezed my hand and bounced a little as my face and classroom appeared on the screen. One of my students came onscreen, described me as "kooky," and the audience laughed. Then, the newscaster hosting the show pulled out the envelope to name the last finalist. I held my breath. He said my name.

It was a blur from there, in the days, weeks and months that followed. From finalist to San Diego County Teacher of the Year on that surreal night — to California Teacher of the Year, to The White House, standing next to President Obama, as he announced the National Teacher of the Year from among four of us who were named finalists. That time, my name was not called, which was a mix of huge relief (by then I had a newborn and a toddler at home with my postpartum wife in California, and I was missing out!) and disappointment (was this surreal journey over?).

As I traveled home from Washington, D.C. that winter in 2009, and in the years since, I've realized one thing for certain: my Teacher of the Year journey, which began at my struggling middle school and took me all the way to the nation's capital and the <u>CBS Evening News</u>, was surely not over.

I had learned so much, met so many amazing people, and experienced so many impactful situations, that I only had MORE to do, and MORE to share going forward. I've also realized that those of us who have had our names called, as "Teacher of the Year" in any arena, have much in common, and much that we can learn and do together. And it's all, at core, in the name of elevating the teaching profession and the state of education in our communities and our nation.

That's where this book begins.

WELCOME TO THE CLUB

Congratulations! If you are reading this book, chances are, you've been chosen as a Teacher of the Year (or some similarly-named award for teaching) — by your state, county, district, school or nation, or by a non-profit or private organization.

You've been recognized as succeeding in what you most likely went into teaching to do — making a difference in the lives of students! You've been singled out as a teacher who is doing something innovative — be it the creative lessons you come up with, the great attitude you bring to a tough teaching environment, or the deep connections you make with your students and colleagues.

Whether you've been recognized at the district level or the state level matters not, what matters is that you have been given a title that — like it or not (and likely you will like it often, though perhaps not-so-much sometimes!) — changes how you are viewed and even what you can do as an educator.

You are now, and always, a Teacher of the Year.

GULP. NOW WHAT?
(START WITH THIS BOOK.)

Does being a Teacher of the Year mean anything, really? Does it change you? Is it just something to put on your resume? Are you expected to DO something now, and in the future? How do you handle this new spotlight? Are these feelings normal? What do other Teachers of the Year do with their awards?

This book aims to help answer these and other questions you likely have as a newly selected Teacher of the Year, to help you navigate your new role — and to connect you with a network of fellow teacher-leaders who are traveling this path with you.

I know that most of us TOYs (the fun acronym for "Teachers of the Year" within teacher-leadership circles) asked questions like those above after we were selected. I also know that most TOYs *are* changed by receiving this kind of award. And they are asked to DO certain things that some are more comfortable with than others — such as interviewing, networking, public speaking, interacting with media, writing our experiences and opinions, and much more.

It just so happens that I am pretty comfortable with a lot of these skills asked of TOYs, having always loved public speaking, having had a career before teaching that built these skills, being married to a former journalist-turned university career counselor, among other reasons. So, after my year "on duty" as a TOY, I began to mentor and help other TOYs learn to navigate the — shall we call them duties? or, better yet, opportunities? — that being a teacher in the spotlight invites.

For the past several years now, I've coached TOYs one-on-one, and I've given group presentations for TOYs in my home state of California, on the skills I mention above. My savvy wife Megan helps me as I help TOYs navigate interviews, write compelling op-eds and speeches, answer journalists' tough questions, and balance the emotions and work-life issues that come with being a teacher-leader in the public eye.

WHAT YOU'LL FIND HERE

You won't find a lot of theory, ideology or a bunch of educational jargon in this book. As a TOY, you probably already know all that stuff. As teachers, we're experts in teaching; yet very few of us are comfortable or trained in giving speeches, networking at social events, and using our platform as a Teacher of the Year to create the change we want to see in education.

What you will find is access to the kind of *professional, outside-the-classroom skills training* I see is needed (and I want to provide!) to help us do the work of elevating our profession and education. The skills I mean aren't teaching, research or policy-making skills (which other organizations do well) — but more of the soft skills of public teacher-leadership, such as networking, platform-building, interviewing, speech-giving, and more. (Yes, even how to market yourself — for the greater good as well as your own!)

This book provides a taste of all the skills training — formal and informal — I've done with TOYs over the past several years. It will walk you through what you can likely expect to experience, and even feel, as a TOY. (And I'll tell you upfront that while I do serious skills training, I also consider this fun, and I hope to make it fun when possible. Joking about self-promotion or awkward cocktail party conversations, for me, makes it all much more palatable!)

You'll also find in this book a collection of experiences and wisdom from many TOYs, from school level on up to National Teachers of the Year — TOYs who are happy to share what they've learned and to support you on your path. When we connect with, support and learn from fellow TOYs, all of us, and the field of education, are stronger for it. Lastly, I've asked some "outside experts" to weigh in with wisdom that can help TOYs thrive in our teacher-leader role.

TOY TALK...

"Be open to the opportunities to spend time with other compassionate TOYs who share your same zeal for teaching. You can learn as much from them as they can from you.

Everyone leaves the year with more ideas, more momentum, and more determination to effect positive social change."

Luajean Bryan, *Tennessee Teacher of the Year*

My hope is that this book can benefit any TOY or teacher-leader wanting to "up your game," navigate the nuts and bolts and larger field of being a teacher-leader in the spotlight, and make a broader difference in education. I wrote this book to help you feel less alone, and more prepared, to leverage your new role and make a bigger difference in the arena of education that matters most to you.

TOY TALK...

"Most likely, you became a TOY because you have aspired to live a life of significance rather than a life of prominence. Now that some prominence has come, use it to live a life of greater significance; both for the profession and for the students you love."

Beth Ekre, *North Dakota Teacher of the Year*

So, without further ado, let's dive in, and take a look at the deepest level of what it is to be a Teacher of the Year.

CHAPTER 2

FACING THE FEELINGS & "THE FACT": YOUR ROLE AS TEACHER OF THE YEAR

Whatever combination of factors led to you be selected as a Teacher of the Year, you can be proud and thrilled to be chosen. Enjoy the feeling! In a profession where we are often not recognized (particularly financially), winning an award like Teacher of the Year is especially gratifying. Let's face it, we didn't go into teaching for the big money, we went into teaching to educate. You are clearly doing that — and more!

Now, I know, you also may be having a little bit of the "Do I deserve this?" guilt and self-doubt coming up. Don't worry, I have yet to meet a Teacher of the Year, at any level, who doesn't at least have a little bit of this. Let's face it: there is always someone who stays at school more hours than us, or has higher test scores, or keeps in better touch with her students, or takes his students on more field trips than us. You know what I mean.

This mixed bag of feelings, when being chosen as Teacher of the Year, is incredibly normal and natural. One of my main motivations for writing this book for others was that it helped me so much to realize other TOYs shared similar feelings and experiences with me. To know I wasn't alone on this somewhat surreal journey.

TOY TALK...

"My best advice would be to enjoy the experience — truly ENJOY the opportunity to meet colleagues of such outstanding caliber.

Time constraints will be challenging and you will be out of your classroom often, but the rewards of knowledge gained and relationships formed will prove invaluable.

The TOY experience is one of growth and will allow you to see education and your role as a teacher in myriad new ways. ENJOY!"

Chantelle Herchenhahn,
Mississippi Teacher of the Year

It was a great relief for me when I learned that my complicated emotions about being a TOY — from being "chosen" to actually living the realities of the title, in my active year and beyond — are feelings experienced by so many fellow TOYs.

I also found it helpful to know at the beginning of this journey that there is one question nearly every TOY has asked: *Am I really the best teacher?*

are you THe BesT TeaCHeR?
(anD WHY IT reaLLY Doesn'T maTTeR.)

How can you compare a kindergarten teacher in the inner-city to a high school AP history teacher in an affluent neighborhood? You can't. So let's start by getting one thing straight: You are *not* the best teacher. I am not the best teacher. Nobody is the best teacher.

You're a great teacher, but being the "best" is impossible to determine. What you are, however, is someone who is a fantastic person to *represent the teaching profession.* Whether you were selected as a Teacher of the Year by your students, colleagues, or by someone in an office somewhere whom you've never met, you are someone who deserves to be recognized for your accomplishments and aspirations.

TOY TALK...

"The title Teacher of the Year is a misnomer, as it implies something that we are not: the nation's best teachers.

We are, however, among the best teachers to advocate for the teaching profession and, more importantly, our students. And we have been given a tremendous opportunity and responsibility to be America's ambassadors of education."

Tony Mullen, *National Teacher of the Year*

For me, a big "a-ha" at the very beginning of my Teacher of the Year journey was the need to own this concept — the "big fact" that I was chosen *to represent teachers.* Representing teachers is a huge opportunity and responsibility. If we can let go of caring about whether we are better or worse teachers than any others (please let this go, even if others around you may not!), and focus on how we can best *represent teachers,* it makes the emotional journey of the TOY much less fraught, and much more fun.

TOY TALK...

"My foremost piece of advice is to remember the beauty of humility. When you become a Teacher of the Year, especially for an entire state, you are instantaneously thrust into the limelight. Cameras flash, the media calls, and suddenly, your previously unheard voice heeded. Amidst all the accolades, pride can easily edge in.

So, remember first that you are representative of an entire profession comprised of literally thousands of educators, heroes in their classrooms on a daily basis, most whom are never formally recognized for their efforts.

Remember the beauty of humility also when you move forward. Life goes on, and new teachers become subsequent years' honorees. Granted, your life will never be the same. Unimaginable opportunities and experiences will be provided, and new doors will be opened. As the years go by, though, I'm finding that allusions to my having been a state Teacher of the Year is a whole lot more palatable coming from others than from me."

Jean Lamar, *Florida Teacher of the Year*

EMBRACE THE STRETCH

On the macro level, that's the big fact: you were chosen to represent teachers. On the micro level, though, you being chosen is a call to *stretch yourself* personally and professionally. The realities of being a TOY include: others will see you differently, some will admire you beyond reason, others will feel threatened or resentful of you beyond reason, you will be put into new situations, you will be asked tough questions, you will be faced with contemplating who you are as an educator and as a person.

The story of every TOY is different — how we were chosen, our backgrounds, our level of local support, our personal lives, our classrooms, what we aim to do (or not do) with this title. But what is the same for every TOY is that *we are all given the opportunity to grow and move beyond the comfort of our classrooms*, and even our anonymity. We can choose to embrace this or shrink from it; it's up to us.

CHRIS HARRIS' STORY

Veteran math teacher Chris Harris was never a fan of the Teacher of the Year hoopla at her school, and always declined being nominated. But then, one year, her attitude toward being a TOY shifted, as she accepted the title of Mission Middle School Teacher of the Year. Here's her story:

"I had a year where everything that I believed about my school 'persona' was shot down by an administrator. I was not the leader I thought I was, I was not the mentor I thought I was, I did not have the school spirit I thought I did, I did not treat students the way I thought I did. It was devastating!

Then, my nomination for Teacher of the Year by a respected colleague (a former TOY himself, who truly admired my work), and the comments from my peers upon hearing of my nomination, gave me just the boost I needed. I confronted the administrator and explained who I was, what I was, and why I was successful. And I did this knowing that I had the support of the people with whom I worked.

It changed my attitude, made me refine my skills, made some others see me in a new light. And it made ME a better teacher."

I hope you will embrace this opportunity to grow as a teacher, a person, and as a representative of our profession. You were chosen for a reason, for your own life — finding the nuance of that reason is something each TOY does for ourselves!

So, now that we've covered some of the more existential stuff, let's move onto the nuts and bolts — the skills and strategies required to successfully navigate the wider world of a TOY.

TOY TALK...

"The best advice I can give to any Teacher of the Year is to be yourself. You were selected for this role because of your unique talents, beliefs, and accomplishments, and the education world needs to learn from you.

There is no single mold for Teacher of the Year, so do not feel pressured to be someone other than yourself. Be proud of what you have accomplished and yet humble enough to recognize the growth you are yet to experience."

Jenna Hallman, *South Carolina Teacher of the Year*

CHAPTER 3

THE TOUGH QUESTIONS:
INTERVIEWS

Chances are, you were interviewed to become a Teacher of the Year, or you'll be interviewed shortly after becoming one, depending on where you are in the process. If you are anything like me, I hadn't sat through an interview since I interviewed for my position to begin my first year of teaching.

Being interviewed can be challenging and fun, and an excellent opportunity to share your ideas. It can also be intimidating and nerve-wracking, as we all fear not having an immediate answer to a question that is asked, or that we'll talk in tangents without ever really answering the questions.

PREPARING FOR INTERVIEWS

Lucky for me, my wife Megan used to present workshops to graduate students on interview preparation at the University of California-San Diego (she also was a teacher at the university), so I had an in-house interview coach as I was preparing for my TOY interviews. Here are three of her interview prep tips that I've found invaluable, as have other TOYs we've passed them on to:

1) **Anticipate questions in advance.**

   You might not be able to predict every question you'll be asked, but anticipating general questions will allow you to formulate the quality of answers you'll give.

You'll usually find that the questions asked are very similar to the questions that you anticipate. Remember: it only takes one "I nailed it" answer to sway an interviewer's decision in your favor. Also, it's OK and ethical to contact a TOY from a previous year, to ask them about their experience with the interview process, and ask them what questions they remember being asked during their interview. (Unless, of course, they are on the selection committee!)

Here are some typical topics you can expect to be asked about in TOY interviews:

✓ Your teaching philosophy

✓ How you engage students

✓ How you work with parents, administrators and community

✓ Your opinion on the biggest problems in education (always end with your ideas for *solutions or actions you have taken* — even if that is not specifically asked!)

✓ How you would represent your (school, district, state, field, etc.)

✓ How you handle challenges (conflict, classroom disruptions)

✓ Your strengths and weaknesses as a teacher (always consider "weaknesses" as your "areas to grow" and explain how you are successfully working on them and making strides)

2) Gather (and practice) your anecdotes.

Interview answers that include anecdotes (you know, "one time, in my classroom...") are almost always the ones interviewers remember most. They are more interesting, and easier to follow, and they allow you to "show not tell"

expert advice...

YOUR INTERVIEW SECRET WEAPON

"My very best interview anecdote — which helped land me a coveted job — was actually about my biggest teaching failure. I told the story of how I was teaching a class on "the history of media" at a university summer institute for senior citizens.

I walked into the first class session and presented a lecture filled with all my academic jargon and theory. It was a complete disaster; the seniors were bored and annoyed. The next day, not one person showed up for my class. I was mortified. I had to think fast and swallow my pride. I walked into the lounge where all the seniors were socializing and announced my apology for the boring class, promised it would be more fun and relevant today, and asked them to please give me another chance. They probably felt sorry for me, so they came back.

I then played a recording of the "War of the Worlds" broadcast and asked them what they remembered about it in their lives. They talked about their memories the whole class time, and it seamlessly connected with bigger issues of media history, without any lecturing from me! Everything shifted, the class became fun and educational for all of us, and they enthusiastically showed up for the rest of the class meetings.

Think about how this kind of story can be applied to any number of questions that may come your way in an interview — how you handle adversity, how you find ways to connect with or engage students, how you shift your lessons to meet students' needs, how you are open to learning, how you think on your feet, etc. Having anecdotes like these, practiced and ready to tell concisely, is a "secret weapon" for interview success!

The moral for interview anecdotes: tell a great story concisely, show your humanity, and end on a positive!"

Megan Pincus Kajitani, *educator &*
former university career counselor

who you are as a teacher (you English teachers know that phrase well!).

Megan always encourages people to take a couple of hours and brainstorm all of the anecdotes that show who you are, your most challenging and your finest moments in your professional and personal life. Jot down all of the interesting things that have happened to you, that can illustrate how you handle obstacles, how you connect with others, how you manage stress, your integrity and your outlook.

Then, pick a good half dozen or more of these anecdotes and practice telling them out loud. This is not something you want to do on the fly — trust me, it is easy to drone on and get off track trying to "wing it" with these kinds of stories. When you say them aloud — even to yourself in the car or in the mirror — you will be able to pull out the main points, recall the best and most relevant details, and refine your stories so that they are enjoyable to hear.

Then, when you practice mock interviews, experiment with using your anecdotes in answers to different anticipated questions. Not every answer needs to include an anecdote, but you definitely want to sprinkle them into your answers as much as you can. It makes a much more fun and memorable experience for the interviewers — which they will greatly appreciate, especially if they are doing many interviews in a row (including mostly people who give broad, theoretical answers!).

3) Practice on video.

I know, this doesn't sound so fun for most of us, but it is so enlightening! When you see yourself answering on video, you get to see how others see you. And for most of us, it is at least slightly different than we think we are coming across.

Yes, it can be a bit disconcerting. You may have no idea how you swat at your bangs, or itch your nose, or take too long to get to the point, or say "um" way too often. BUT, don't let this make you more self-conscious, use it as an opportunity to be aware and make adjustments!

After you've practiced on video once, do a few practice sessions without the video — using what you've seen and learned — THEN, videotape it again. You WILL see improvements, and this is a great confidence boost.

ACING INTERVIEWS

If you've practiced well, you can walk in knowing you are prepared and simply approach the interview as a conversation. That's really what an interview at this level is: just a conversation with other professionals in your field.

Here are some tips to make your "conversation" a success — to help you be an "interviewee of the year":

ALEX KAJITANI'S SEVEN STRATEGIES FOR INTERVIEW SUCCESS

1) **Know who is interviewing you, and what organization they represent.**

    Whenever possible, find out in advance who will be sitting on the interview committee, or what organization they work for. A simple internet search should reveal enough information for you to work with.

    In addition, knowing something about the people/organization interviewing you shows them that you are well-informed, and gives you the opportunity to ask questions about the work they are doing.

2) Walk in confidently, smiling and making eye contact.

Enough said. It's a must. Let's move on to #3.

3) Work the room.

Often, an interview committee will consist of several people sitting in the same room, with each person taking turns asking a different question. Avoid the natural tendency to answer *only* the person who asked the question. Instead, when answering each question, attempt to make eye contact with each person on the committee.

An easy way to remember to do this is to begin by looking at the person who asked the question, and make your way clockwise or counter-clockwise around the room. Try your best to finish your answer while looking at the person who asked the question. By including everyone in your answer, you shift the interview from a "question and answer" format to more of a "conversation" with you as the leader!

4) Plan your closing.

Most interviews will end with the final question being something like, "Finally, is there anything else that you would like to tell us about yourself?" or, "Are there any questions that you have for us?" Regardless, this is an invitation for you to put the final touches on your interview.

You can use this time to ask clarifying questions, but after you get the answers you need, you can still launch into your closing statement. Don't be humble! Whatever you need the interview committee to know, put it out there. Know in advance what you are going to say, and practice it in advance so that you say it with confidence and grace.

Even if one of the interview questions asked you to relate information that you planned on using in your closing, you can simply say, "I want to reiterate something that came up, because I believe it is so important to know about me…" Really important: do everything in your power to end with good energy, on a POSITIVE note.

5) Remember that confidence, smile and eye contact you walked in with?

Walk out with it as well. Even if you don't think the interview went well, walk out as if it did (you don't know how badly the person before you did!).

6) Record the questions.

As soon as you can after your interview (like when you get back to your car or classroom), write down as many of the interview questions that you can remember, as well as how you answered them.

There is a high likelihood that you will be asked that exact question (or something very similar) again in the future. If you answered it well: write it down so you can replicate it. If you struggled to answer it: write it down so you can improve upon it.

Rarely have I walked out of an interview and not thought of the perfect answer to a question after it was too late. Write it down so you can nail it the next time!

7) Send a thank you note.

Whenever possible, send a thank you note immediately after your interview. Read more about the why's and how's of thank you notes — including a great post-interview thank-you note story! — in the next chapter.

My final note on interviews is to reiterate the idea of thinking of them as *a conversation among professionals*. Remember, you are a professional, and you were chosen to interview because someone thought you were doing something interesting! Tap into your joy of teaching, and let it shine through.

Too many people psyche themselves out about interviews, and it's really a waste of energy. Channel your energy into sharing with the interviewers what you love to share with your students — your passion for your work is what they are looking for, and if you focus on that and do your prep, interviews can actually be fun!

TOY TALK...

"Be true to yourself! Remember to be who you are, not who someone would have you be, or a new you imagined by those you meet along your path and journey. By doing so, you will enjoy the year and best represent the unique dynamics of education."

Jen Haberling, *Michigan Teacher of the Year*

CHAPTER 4

IT'S THE LITTLE THINGS:
BUSINESS CARDS
& THANK YOU NOTES

As Teachers of the Year, two of the most effective tools we have come in very small boxes: business cards and thank you notes.

This may seem a trivial thing to be talking about but, please, hear me out. These "little things" can make a *big* difference for your success in making connections (which helps you make a bigger difference!) as a TOY. I am a huge advocate of paying attention to, and making use of, business cards and thank you notes — and I know that doing so has allowed me to open doors that would've surely stayed closed otherwise.

BUSINESS CARDS: NOT FOR THE TRASH!

Recently, I attended a dinner where I met another Teacher of the Year. After chatting for a while, we exchanged business cards, and I told him I'd really like to stay in touch. As he handed me his business card, he said, "I gotta admit; whenever somebody gives me their business card, there's a pretty good chance it ends up lost or in the trash by the end of the night."

As I walked to my car, I was dismayed by this comment. Here was a Teacher of the Year, missing out on the value of building connections, or staying in touch. As teachers, we're often so wrapped up in what's happening inside the walls of our classrooms, we give little thought to building community beyond those walls.

If you don't have business cards provided for you, you can easily and cheaply order them. Be sure to include your organization's name followed by "Teacher of the Year." Be sure that "Teacher of the Year" is displayed prominently on your business card, along with your website, blog and/or social media handles (if you have them), your email address and other contact information.

You'll be surprised at how many people glance at your card and see "Teacher of the Year" and suddenly get much friendlier and more interested in you. Here again, it's great to call on the fact that you were given this title to represent teachers and contribute to our profession — let your title open doors and then walk through them to do something positive for education!

★ ALEX KAJITANI'S SEVEN STEPS TO BUSINESS CARD SUCCESS

I take business cards very seriously. When someone hands me their business card, I see it as an invitation to connect, to stay in touch, and maybe even be friends. In this day and age, staying in touch is very easy, due to social media, texting and email. At the same time, it is also very difficult, due to all of the people, products and information competing for our attention.

I also love to create systems and lists (and name them after myself!). So, here is a seven-step system I designed to ensure that when someone hands you their business card, they become available to work with you for a long time to come:

Step 1: Upon being handed a business card, glance at it (use this time to find their name, if you didn't catch it the first time around), and notice the company, title, etc. If I like the look of it, I'll even say something like, "Cool card!"

Step 2: Give them your card (Steps 1 and 2 can also be done in reverse).

Step 3: Place card in your pocket (OK, that's obvious, but this ensures that it doesn't end up lost or in the trash!). My wife, Megan, carries a felt business card pouch in her purse and puts them all in there to not lose them.

Step 4: If necessary, when you have a free moment, jot down notes on the back of the card, such as what you talked about, something memorable, or any pertinent information you need to remember.

Step 5: Go home and send them a "nice to meet you" card (see prompt on the next page). Stock cards on typical stationary are OK, but also consider using a custom card that they won't discard immediately; something with a great photo or inspiring quote on it. I know it seems like a lot of work to write this card, but it only takes about two minutes, and only costs the price of a card and stamp. That's a pretty cheap price to ensure that someone remembers you forever.

Step 6: File the business card somewhere accessible. Heck, even throw it in a shoebox. But keep that shoebox where you can access it (and somewhere you won't mistakenly throw it away). San Diego County TOY Jo-Ann Fox takes an iPhone photo of all of her business cards and stores them in an app made for that purpose — a great tip for the tech-savvy!

Step 7: Know that you might not hear back from them. Don't be offended. Most people don't do these kinds of things, so why would they have a protocol for responding? By sending the card, you have opened your own door to them. You are now free to contact them should you need their assistance, advice or partnership. And, trust me on this: when you do, they remember you! From time to time, when you come across an article that makes you think of them, email it to them. Or go old school, and cut it out and mail it to them. People LOVE that!

I can honestly say I think this small practice of mine is one of my top "secrets of success" in my career. I'm happy to share it with you, and I hope you will take advantage of the connections it will bring your way.

SaMPLe PROMPT FOR a "nICe TO MeeT YOU" CaRD:

Dear Matt:

It was a pleasure meeting you at the Title 1 Conference last week. I really enjoyed exchanging ideas about connecting with unmotivated students. I hope our paths cross again in the future!

Best Wishes,
Alex Kajitani
California Teacher of the Year

THe WHeN'S, WHY'S anD HOW'S OF THanK YOU nOTes

We all likely remember being nagged by our parents to write thank you notes for gifts received. Perhaps we nag our kids to write them, too. And with good reason: people appreciate being appreciated! In a professional sense, thank you notes (like "nice to meet you notes") may be a lot less common than they used to be — which is all the more reason to utilize them to stand out as someone who cares (which I'm sure you do!).

WHEN to send a thank you note?

After an interview (immediately after! Do not pass Go, do not collect $200!). After someone meets you for tea or a meal (no matter who paid, thank them for their time and company). After a speaking opportunity. When someone does something nice for you, like recommends you for that speaking opportunity, or that book chapter, etc.

WHY to send a thank you note?

In all cases, there are two main reasons:

1) It's a polite and classy thing to do.

2) It leaves an impression on people that you are gracious and thoughtful (which, of course, you are!).

ALEX'S STORY

"As a Top-4 Finalist for National Teacher of the Year, I flew to Washington, D.C. to interview with a (um, somewhat intimidating) committee of education leaders. I sent a thank you note to as many of the committee members as possible.

Although the nation's top teaching honor ultimately went to someone else, one of the committee members, who was the editor-in-chief for the *American School Boards Journal* (ASBJ) called a few months later, asking if he could interview me for ASBJ's monthly magazine. They ended up running a full-page feature story on the work I was doing!"

In the case of interviews, there are two more reasons:

1) If you were selected, the thank you note will confirm for the committee that they made the right choice.

2) If you were not selected, the thank you note will ensure that they remember you for a long time, and will think of you for future opportunities.

HOW to write a thank you note? Not sure what to say?

Simple and gracious is all you need. No need to get fancy about it. It's nice to add a small specific about something you discussed, to seal the connection. Here's an example of what I say*:

> *Dear Ms. Josephson:*
>
> *It was a pleasure meeting you during the Teacher of the Year interviews yesterday. I truly appreciated the opportunity to discuss my ideas on education, and certainly hope that our paths cross again in the future.*
>
> *All the Best,*
> *Alex Kajitani*
>
> *Be sure to include your business card with the note!

I have a small box of thank you notes and stamps that I keep in the car, because I know the value of sending that thank you note right away. It impresses people and ensures that they don't forget me — and it ensures that I don't forget to write my thank you notes!

In short, business cards and thank you notes are little things that can have a big impact on your ability to connect with people and open doors — enjoy them and *use* them.

CHAPTER 5

WHO ARE YOU?:
BUILDING YOUR PLATFORM

{
definition

Platform: *A declaration of the principles on which a person or group of persons stands.*
}

Picture this: You're giving a speech to a crowded room full of people. They're all sitting in chairs, and you're standing in front of them, on the same floor their chairs are on. The people in the first few rows can see you; however, you notice that beyond those rows, people are having trouble seeing you. They're craning their necks, and trying to look around the people in front of them. If they're lucky, they can see your face. As a result of not being able to see you, they have trouble paying attention, and are not able to receive the full impact of your talk.

Now, picture the same scenario; however, this time you're up on a stage. Everyone in the room can see you, and you can see them. As a result, everyone effortlessly sees and hears your message, and your speech has much more of an impact on the crowd. The only difference between the two scenarios is that in the second, you have something to stand on — *a platform.*

I find this concept of a literal platform helpful in thinking about the figurative platform that can help us be most effective as Teachers of the Year. The idea is having something to stand on — or stand for — that people can identify us with, and that helps us target a certain issue in education we can work to improve.

WHY TO HAVE A PLATFORM

Non-fiction writers, politicians, speakers and other professionals identify their platforms to help them build audiences and build support for their causes. A platform today is seen as a combination of your cause, your message, and your brand; in a way, it is your public identity. As TOYs, your platform will be related to education — more specifically, to something you are passionate about or experienced with in education.

As a Teacher of the Year, you don't have to know everything about everything in education. However, you do have an opportunity to use your voice to help create change that is positive for the profession. As a TOY, *people want to hear what you have to say*! However, while telling stories and advocating for the profession is great, having a common theme that guides your decisions and actions will ultimately make you much more successful, effective and memorable.

First of all, *you can make much more headway on your cause* (really another way to think about platform) if you are intentional about it, and weave it through the work you are doing as a TOY. When you choose a platform to stand on, this is what journalists will write about when they interview you, what audiences will want to hear you speak about, and what people will seek you out to be a part of. Your passion within education will have a much better chance at being noticed — and thus you will be able to make a bigger difference — if you identify it as your platform and use it as such.

Secondly, knowing your platform also *makes your job as a TOY easier*. When you are asked to give a speech, write an op-ed, participate in a conference panel, or be interviewed, it sure is easier to have something to focus on and talk about that is meaningful to you. It also prevents others from creating an image of you *for* you! You have more control, center and intention if you identify your own platform.

TOY TALK ...

"With the accolades comes influence. Use it to stand up for that which you believe is right. There are many students being underserved, there are many peers in need of our help, there are many schools which could use some good ol' fashioned TLC.

Being a TOY provides an amazing opportunity to BE OF SERVICE. You can't be everything to everybody but you will certainly be vested with the power to be something to somebody. Smile, work hard and give!"

Alan Sitomer,
California Teacher of the Year

HOW TO IDENTIFY YOUR PLATFORM

So, you may be thinking, how exactly do I identify my platform?

Chances are, you were selected as a Teacher of the Year because there is something that sets you apart from other teachers. Something that you have devoted a significant amount of time to, or that you have gotten particularly good at.

Thus, the first step to building your platform is to answer the following question: *As a teacher, what are you all about?*

If you are having trouble answering this question, consider the following questions:

1) If you could realistically work to change anything in education, what would you change?

2) As a teacher, what do you believe in the most?

3) If you could help other teachers become GREAT at something, what would that be?

Your platform can be one or two causes that intersect; more than three typically gets too confusing. However, you can always have sub-themes within your platform. For example, my original TOY platform involved two issues: closing the achievement gap and math literacy. My sub-theme within that platform is incorporating culturally relevant curriculum, which includes talking about ethnicity as well as using rap music to engage students in academic learning.

TOY TALK ...

"My advice for any future Teacher of the Year would be to speak tirelessly on behalf of an underserved group in our society.

Find an oppressed group with whom you identify and give voice to the challenges they face, their perceptions on how the educational system (or society in general) underserves or ignores them, and offer solutions that might be implemented to address these concerns."

Michael Love, *San Diego County Teacher of the Year*

Examples of other Teacher of the Year platforms I've seen:

- Providing education for homeless children
- Lowering high school dropout rates
- Keeping arts education in the schools
- Encouraging a love of reading

Take some time and write out your platform — how you want to serve the field of education and in what arena you want to make an impact with your attention as a Teacher of the Year.

TOY TALK ...

"When named Teacher of the Year, the overwhelming time concerns, commitments and responsibilities to the position require developing a clear, convincing, and consistent stance.

Pay attention to both the big picture and the all important details. Develop three points or themes well, each focused on how educators make our world a better place on a daily basis."

MaryLu Hutchins, *West Virginia Teacher of the Year*

HOW TO MAKE THE MOST EFFECTIVE USE OF YOUR PLATFORM

Once you've identified your platform, take every opportunity to build it, promote it, and create a community around it that can help you. Having an effective platform helps you become very visible, especially in a world where every great idea is competing with millions of other great ideas; often on the same laptop screen. It also allows you to connect with others who have similar interests, and to form partnerships with those who can help you continue to build on your work.

TOY TALK ...

"I always recommend distilling your message down to something that can be described in one or two words: Equality. Balance. Creativity. 21st Century Skills. Engagement. Professionalism. These words are pretty

(continued on next page)

TOY TALK *(continued)* ...

tough to argue with, and can provide a jumping off point for any answer, speech, article, or cocktail party conversation.

I think almost all of my talks centered around the idea of Balance: balance between creative and analytical thinking; balance between humility and confidence; balanced legislation; balanced assessments; balanced evaluation methods of teachers; balance between work and life.

Whenever someone asked me a question about anything and I felt tongue-tied, I'd start out with 'balance' and go from there. It works well to have a 'go-to' word."

Michael Geisen, *National Teacher of the Year*

Here are a few tips to help you most effectively utilize your platform:

1) **Create an elevator pitch**. According to Wikipedia, an elevator pitch is:

> "A short summary used to quickly and simply define a product, service, or organization and its value proposition. The name 'elevator pitch' reflects the idea that it should be possible to deliver the summary in the time span of an elevator ride, or approximately thirty seconds to two minutes."

Once you have your elevator pitch, you will learn quickly to use it in all the situations being a TOY puts you in — from cocktail parties to conferences. (See the Networking and Conferences chapters for more on this.) After you give your elevator pitch, people who hear it should be able to describe you as "The teacher who ___(fill in your platform)___."

2) **Ask for support for your cause.** Remember, most people love teachers. They understand that teachers work very hard for not a lot of money, and they also remember fondly one of the teachers they had as a child. As a result, many people will want to help you in your cause. So, use your platform to make a difference — by getting others on board!

The only hitch: *You have to ask for it.* When you ask, be direct and unapologetic about what you need. This doesn't mean to be pushy or aggressive, but you do need to state what it is that you need, and leave the responsibility of saying "no" on them.

I've asked for everything from free food catering for events we've held, to supplies donations from supply stores, and even legal services. Sometimes I got them, and other times I didn't. In short, understanding that your Teacher of the Year status opens doors to promoting your platform is ethical, effective, and quite honestly, the only way you're going to truly get anything done.

3) **Use your platform to say "No."** As a TOY, you will be asked to support causes, promote products, and give testimonials. As teachers, we often want to help everyone. If you are asked to support something that you truly believe in, by all means, do it. However, if you are unsure or uninterested in lending your support, your own platform can be a great way to say "no."

Consider saying something like, "I'm really sorry, but my platform is ___(fill in your platform)___, and I only support causes that link directly with the work that I'm doing." Or, "I am putting all of my energy into working on the cause of ___(fill in your platform)___, so I'm afraid I'll have to pass — but thank you for the opportunity!"

Not only does this give you a chance to say "no" in a respectful and honest manner, it also allows you to inform them of the work you're doing, and ensure that they think of you the next time they come across a news story or another person whose work does fit your platform!

A platform doesn't have to define you *forever*. It evolves over time (for example, my own is becoming about developing teacher-leaders!). But choosing a platform as a TOY helps your focus and impact tremendously.

Lastly, I encourage you to GO FOR IT with your TOY platform! Those dreams you have of making a true impact on education? Now's the time to make them a reality! Think big, think deep, and you never know what you can accomplish.

TOY TALK ...

"Be bold and be prepared. This is the time to think big and bold. You will have incredible opportunities to meet influencers and decision-makers.

Know what you want for teaching and learning, make it be something meaningful and innovative, and have clearly defined talking points to share your ideas with people who can help make them happen."

Katherine Bassett, *Executive Director, National Network of State Teachers of the Year (NNSTOY), and New Jersey Teacher of the Year*

CHaPTeR 6

"PLeQSe WeLcome...":
GIVING SPeecHes

As a Teacher of the Year, you will be asked to give speeches. To some, giving speeches is an adrenaline rush that is welcome. To others, sweaty visions of 7th grade English class create an urge to vomit. Either way, you've been selected to speak on behalf of the teaching profession, so let's talk about giving speeches.

There are really two steps to giving speeches: crafting your speech, and delivering your speech. While intimately interrelated, these two steps also take two different skill sets, so I like to address them separately.

CRaFTING a GReaT SPeecH

If you haven't already, be sure to read the previous chapter on Building Your Platform, because having a clear platform — a cause you stand for — makes it much easier to know what to focus on when crafting your speech. So, knowing your platform helps you select a topic for your speech (some angle of your platform) — and then you have your topic. Now what?

Of course, there are entire books and careers dedicated to the art of crafting speeches. You can pick up those books if speech-writing is something you want to dive deeply into. For now, however, for the sake of survival as you launch your Teacher of the Year speaking tour, I'll just offer you a few speech-crafting nuggets (another self-named system!) that have helped me in this arena.

⭐ ALEX KAJITANI'S EIGHT GREAT STRATEGIES FOR SPEECH-CRAFTING SUCCESS

1) **Have different versions of the same speech.** You'll save yourself a lot of time and energy if you don't have to write a new speech every time you are asked to speak. Have several versions of the same speech, such as a one-minute, five-minute and 15-minute version. You may even be asked to speak for an hour or more!

   Of course, your different versions may vary in their content and messages, but one way to ease the speechwriting process is to have a powerful opening and closing, and, depending on the length of your speech, add or subtract from the middle of your speech depending on the time and audience.

2) **Don't EVER start your speech by saying, "I'm not much of a speech person," or "I'm so nervous up here."** Either of these statements will immediately turn your audience off, and undermine your authority as a Teacher of the Year. If you need to, go Stuart Smalley (did I just age myself by referring to this *Saturday Night Live* character?) and repeat a mantra in your head before you speak: *I am confident, funny, and interesting.* Or whatever you need to tell yourself — just don't tell your audience anything that makes them doubt that they want to listen to you.

   I just mentioned a powerful opening — what might that look like? Something that grabs your audience, in either a bold or subtle way, depending on your personality. This could be a joke, an anecdote, a visual, a statement — find something compelling to begin with. The way I begin the speech that eventually became my TED Talk is by making a bold statement, with a touch of tongue-in-cheek: "I'm Alex Kajitani, and I'm on a mission to make math cool!"

Find what works for you, but try to grab your audience from the get-go.

3) **Use bookends.** Whatever it is you figure out to grab your audience with as an opener, come back around to that at the end of your speech. There is something completely satisfying in listening to a speaker round her topic back to where she started — with a whole new meaning to that opening statement after we've heard the middle of her speech.

There's the old saying: *tell 'em what you're gonna tell 'em, tell 'em, and tell 'em what you told 'em.* And I mean this, but also something more. Did you ever watch comedian Ellen DeGeneres' stand-up routine *Here and Now*? If you get a chance (and would like a little levity and a great break from the intensity of TOY duties), I recommend it as a fabulous example of bookends. Her comedic routine starts out on a topic, winds around all over the map, and somehow comes perfectly back to where she started. It's a brilliantly crafted speech, really (and includes another great speech-crafting strategy: *use humor!*).

In short, think about ways to end on as powerful a note as your started, and to relate your ending back to your beginning. I end my speech by repeating the same line I open with — simple, yet it works as a powerful opening and closing.

4) **Tell stories.** Tell stories about your students. About your successes and failures as a teacher. About the challenges we face every single day as educators. Not only do people love to hear stories, a great story is memorable for a long time after it's told. Stories make us laugh, cry, or think deeply.

As teachers, we tell stories all the time. We tell them in the teachers' lounge; we tell them around the dinner table, and we tell them to our students. As a profession, we are good storytellers. Real stories will help you immediately connect with your audience, as many of them will have experienced the issues you're talking about. Of course, don't overdo it with the stories; just enough to make your point!

What makes a great story? There are no rules, requirements, or expectations that go into telling to a great story. We can tell a story to someone who laughs out loud, then tell the exact story again 15 minutes later to someone who is saddened by it. Either way, though, the key is that they were *affected* by it.

Great stories often contain the following elements:

✓ They tell of how we overcame adversity. As humans, rarely is anything more inspiring than hearing about how someone triumphed after a hard struggle. I heard a speaking coach once say that the key arc is: *mess, turning point, success.*

✓ They begin by highlighting the specific actions of certain individuals, then make the connection to how those actions relate to the "big picture."

✓ They begin by talking about the "big picture," then back this up by highlighting the specific actions of certain individuals.

✓ They are real. Your audience will know, even if subconsciously, when your story belongs to you and is truly in your heart. You can tell other people's stories, as long as you name them as such. A real story touches our hearts, because it comes from the storyteller's heart.

If you've already read and followed the Interviewing chapter, then you've compiled a list of your life and work anecdotes, or stories — the times you triumphed over adversity, the situations that made an impact on you. (If you haven't, check that chapter for the section on "anecdotes" and complete the exercise — it comes in handy in myriad ways and situations!) Now, go back to those stories you dug out of your memory banks, and see if and how they fit into your speech and your platform.

5) **Consider your audience.** When you are crafting your speech, ask yourself who your primary audience will be — teachers, administrators, students, policy-makers, etc.? This makes a huge difference, and you may also need different versions of your "main speech" for these various audiences.

For example, policy-makers and business-people who are not in the classroom need more stories about students and "what it's really like" in schools today. Whereas, fellow teachers know all this, and are more in need of new perspectives, ideas or strategies — or insight on "big ideas" in education you've been exposed to as a TOY — that will help them succeed in their classrooms. Take your audience's needs and perspective into account.

6) **Talk like you teach.** Your teaching is what got you named a TOY, so use what you do with your students with your audiences. Be the teacher you are in the classroom, not just another speaker. Are you interactive? Do you use music? Do you play games? Do you show crazy visuals? Incorporate these elements into your speeches, and audiences (just like your students) will be much happier to listen and learn from you.

7) **Refine, refine, refine.** These tips should help you create the basic foundation of your great stories, and your great speech. Once you've got your speech down on paper (or on screen), practice it aloud, tape yourself if it helps, or practice it in front of a trusted peer or mentor. And don't be afraid to move things around, add and cut, edit away.

My go-to speech has been refined dozens of times — I've added visuals I've found, trimmed down stories that ran too long, reworked awkward phrases.

In the following section on speech delivery, I talk more about getting clues about what to refine as we are speaking. This is that intimate interrelation of speech craft and delivery I mentioned before — and it's about coming back to speech-crafting, even after delivering your speech, as much as needed until your speech feels tight and impactful with every word.

8) **Always make sure that the last two words of our speech are "Thank You!"** It's gracious, and it cues the audience that you're finished.

TOY TALK ...

"When speaking in public or private, whether to one person, a small group, or a large group of people, choose your words carefully. Your title gives your words greater power.

You are now considered a quotable authority on education. Don't be afraid of this power, but embrace it for the greater good of education."

Bill Kvitli, *San Diego County Teacher of the Year*

DELIVERING A GREAT SPEECH

Now, delivery is in some ways a craft, too, but I think of it more as an art form. Your delivery is about your style, your personality, your voice and intonation. And, as I've found to be incredibly important: It's also about your nuts-and-bolts preparation.

So, my top survival strategies for TOYs, to help you deliver your speeches from your best, contain nuggets on both preparation (before you give your speech) and your actual delivery.

★ aLeX KaJITaNI's
SeVen GOLDen RULeS
FOR GReaT SPeeCH DeLiVeRY

1) **Get as many details in advance about the speech you'll be giving.** Some essential pieces of information you'll need are:

    ✓ Date, time and location of the speech.

    ✓ Are you the only one speaking, or are you part of a larger event?

    ✓ How many will be in attendance?

    ✓ How the room will be set up (will you have a microphone, a podium, can you show presentation slides, videos, audio? in what arrangement will people be seated?)

    And don't be afraid to ask for resources: "Can you please make sure that there is a pen and a small pad of paper for each person? Thanks!"

2) **When possible, get to the location early, and get a sense of the room you'll be speaking in.** Check your audio/visual equipment. Stand on the stage and visualize the seats full of people. This will help cut down on nervousness!

3) **Never underestimate the size of the crowd.** The first time I ever gave a speech as a teacher, it was to four people in the back room of our district office. One of the four people in attendance was our district superintendent, who enjoyed my speech so much that she invited me to speak at the next board meeting. Long story short — after that, the crowds got bigger and bigger for each of my speeches.

You never know when something you say will resonate with someone in the crowd. Treat every crowd as if they are the most important crowd you've ever spoken to, and even if you've already given the same speech multiple times, remember that to most people in the audience, it's the first time they've had a chance to hear your ideas.

4) **ALWAYS be ready to speak — even when someone tells you that you won't be speaking.** As a TOY, you'll be invited to various events. Often, the event coordinator who contacts you will tell you that you won't be speaking. However, consider this your warning: *when people find out you're the Teacher of the Year, you'll get "called out," and in an instant, the room will be focused on you, with eager people expecting you to say something.* ALWAYS be ready to speak.

5) **Act as if.** This relates back to the "never start with a negative statement" strategy from the last section. It's about exuding confidence, even if you need to "act it" just a bit. Act as if you are a confident speaker. Act as if you have something inspiring to say. Act as if you are totally comfortable making eye contact with audience members. Act as if you are not flustered when your technology goes wonky. Act as if you are used to being in front of people (which, by the way, you are — being in front of your students every day — so, if it helps, act as if your audience is simply your students!).

For most of us, when we "act as if," we are soon "being" those things when we speak. (If your nerves are debilitating, however, it might be time to get some help from someone: a Toastmasters speaking coach, even an acupuncturist.) If you know you need more help than these simple strategies, don't hesitate to ask for it!

6) **Pay attention to what works.** Is the audience laughing when you expect them to laugh? Are they crying when you're telling a sad story? Did they "get" that line when you delivered it with a certain inflection? If you're not getting the desired reaction, be honest with yourself and change it. A great speech is a living thing, evolving and changing — don't think of it as static and completed, but as a work in progress that you are always improving each time you deliver it.

If you're speaking at a conference-type event and attendees are filling out evaluation forms, ask the event coordinator to forward you any comments (both positive and negative) about your presentation. Remember, you can't please everyone; but you can pay attention to what's working, and what isn't.

7) **Don't be offended by people texting or typing while you're speaking.** That's just the way it is these days; everyone is staring at their phones while driving (which I do NOT recommend!), walking and just about everything else. As a speaker it can be flustering, but we just have to get used to it. We also have to realize that it can actually be a *positive* reaction to our speech!

Once, I saw a young woman who seemed to be texting throughout my conference presentation. Afterward, she came up to me and said, "Your speech was amazing. I was texting all my friends at this conference that they had to come to this room and hear you!" (So glad I didn't call it out — and now I never will!) Especially the younger crowd is used to announcing the play-by-play of their lives on social media, and they may just be Tweeting about your great speech. I like to assume the best with this new social norm now, though it admittedly still feels odd sometimes.

GREAT SPEECHES TO WATCH

I've found one of the greatest resources for studying great speeches in a realistic, modern way (as in, we're not all going to deliver MLK's "I Have a Dream") to be TED Talks.

If you don't know TED Talks, I highly recommend Googling the term, or going directly to TED.com. Note that not all TED Talks are featured on that site; some are found on YouTube only, as TED. com features only select Talks from its many TEDx conferences around the globe.

In short, TED Talks are 15-18-minute speeches where people present their "ideas worth spreading." Having watched many of them, and having had the opportunity to give one myself, I've found that TED Talks showcase our best efforts to present ideas in concise, compelling, and modern ways.

Here are a few TED Talks I most enjoy watching for inspiration and ideas — for both speech-crafting and delivery. (Though, careful not to compare yourself! Again, you're not MLK or Sir Ken Robinson — you're you, but you can be inspired by the craft and delivery of these great speakers!)

1) **Sir Ken Robinson**, *"Schools Kill Creativity"* (http://www.ted.com/talks/ken_robinson_says_schools_ kill_creativity.html)

2) **Zoe Weil**, *"The World Becomes What You Teach"* (www.youtube.com/watch?v=t5HEV96dIuY)

3) **Elizabeth Gilbert**, *"On Nurturing Creative Genius"* (http://www.ted.com/talks/elizabeth_gilbert_on_genius. html)

And then there's my humble TED Talk: **Alex Kajitani,** "Making Math Cool" (http://www.youtube.com/watch?v=rVR6Usd0usY) (I warn you: it includes my less-than-cool dancing!)

There are countless TED Talks to watch and search through. Here are a few lists to help you find some of the best ones to inspire you for your TOY speaking gig crafting and delivery. (Some are even great to show students!)

- http://blog.simplek12.com/education/top-ten-education-ted-talks/

- http://edudemic.com/2012/03/25-ted-talks-perfect-for-classrooms/

- http://www.teachthought.com/trends/10-of-the-best-tedtalks-on-improving-education/

- http://www.newyorker.com/online/blogs/culture/2012/07/five-key-ted-talks.html

CHAPTER 7

COCKTAIL PARTIES & TABLES FOR TEN: NETWORKING A ROOM

As teachers, networking is not a part of our training, and is even looked down upon in our field by many. I know when I used to hear the word "networking," I always envisioned rooms full of real estate agents and pharmaceutical representatives slickly jabbering away, as if they were born with the gift. We are teachers, serious educators, who work very hard, log long hours for little pay, are responsible for educating the children of our nation — we don't have time for *schmoozing*, right?

Trust me, I hear you. (And, yes, I'm poking fun at our professional holier-than-thou-ness a bit.) However, as a TOY who has by now been invited to countless networking events like cocktail parties and dinners, I've also come to truly value the connections I've made in these kinds of situations. Are they my favorite thing to do? No. But, have I found ways to make them productive and enjoyable? Yes, I actually have. And that's what I hope to share with you in this chapter.

CONQUERING COCKTAIL PARTIES

OK, I have to admit something: Nobody feels more out of place at a cocktail party than I do. The reason why — *I don't drink.* Not a drop. But that doesn't mean that I can't grab some carrot sticks and a club soda and make the most of it.

47

As teachers, we're used to being in our classrooms, and as a result, our first instinct is often to avoid places like cocktail parties — and, if we must go to one, we are likely to find someone we know, sit comfortably at a table, and relax. However, as a Teacher of the Year, doing this means we will miss opportunities to meet others, and they miss an opportunity to meet *us*!

I know, that sounds a bit egocentric; however, people really do want to meet inspiring, award-winning teachers! They *love* coming home and telling their spouse, "I met the Teacher of the Year!" And, I've actually found after enough cocktail parties, that I look forward to meeting people as well — I've now made cocktail party connections that have led to great career opportunities and even friendships!

That doesn't mean you need to be buzzing around the room like a bee, masterfully engaging and impressing everyone in your flight path. It just means make the effort. Connect with old friends, and introduce yourself to some new ones, take it one person at a time (but not just one person!).

TOY TALK ...

"LISTEN to all the people you will meet. The amount of 'social capital' you will acquire is astounding. Many of these people have so much wisdom, such varied experiences, and different viewpoints from your own. If you listen and ask questions, that knowledge can become part of your experience.

LEARN from your experience by keeping a journal that you reflect on each week and what you can take from it. So much will happen so quickly, it will be hard to recall it all a year later.

SHARE everything you learn with your colleagues and do your best to make them part of your journey of learning."

Cindy Couchman, *Kansas Teacher of the Year*

making conversation

I've learned that what most teachers are most uncomfortable with about cocktail parties is trying to make "small talk"— which really means starting and ending brief conversations with people we don't know. Once you have some simple strategies, and lines to start and close with, it gets a whole lot easier.

Here are two simple and genuine lines for opening a conversation:

- "Hi! I haven't met you yet. I'm _____."

- "Hi! I'm _____. Are you a teacher as well?"

After your introduction, I've found the key to cocktail party conversation to be asking interesting questions. People enjoy being listened to, not talked at (just ask our students, right?). Of course, share about your own work — and your platform! — but keep it concise, and be sure to give your conversation partner equal, if not more, time to share.

Networking expert Allison Graham, author of *From Business Cards to Business Relationships*, advises that a cocktail party conversation should last *between three and eight minutes* — and definitely no more than ten! Keeping this in mind can help you keep your pace and know when to transition the conversation to a close. Graham posits that while most of us feel rude ending a conversation, the conventions of networking events actually make it rude to *not* end the conversation, as talking too long would monopolize the other person's time. She created a "Verbal Disengage Formula" that goes:

Transition Word
+ (Name)
+ Relevant Statement
+ (Next Step)

A transition word would be something like "Well" or "So" — that subtly shifts the tone toward ending the conversation. Use the person's name if you caught it. A relevant statement is a recap or compliment that further cues the conversation is coming to a close, such as "It's been great talking with you." And then, you can add a next step — but *only* if you truly plan to follow up — such as, "I'll be happy to email you that article. Do you have a business card?"

So, an example of Graham's formula would go like this:

"Well, Susana, I've enjoyed talking with you. I'd love to get your card so I can send you that website."

Here are two more simple and genuine lines for closing a conversation that I use successfully myself:

- "It was nice meeting you. Let's stay in touch — do you have a business card?" (See Business Cards chapter for more on this!)

- "Here's my card — let me know how I can help you in the future."

Another great closer is introducing your conversation companion to someone else nearby, whom you think they would connect well with. Bottom line, once you smooth out a few openers and closers, these 5-minute-ish conversations are no problem!

Be Ready For These Questions

As a TOY, people will also have questions for *you*. Some will have a few questions; and others will have *quite a few* questions. However, over time, you'll notice that there are certain questions that seem to come up over and over.

You may not answer a question perfectly (or even decently) the first time you're asked. But you can make sure that the second

alex's advice...

DEALING WITH THE "AWKWARD SILENCE"

Yep, silence at a networking event can be awkward. It doesn't mean that *you* are awkward, or a bad networker. It just means that you don't know the person/people you're chatting with well enough.

The best advice I can give you in this situation is to ask them a question. I try to keep questions related to our profession or the event we're attending — always safer than getting personal right away!

Here are six questions I recommend for breaking the awkward silence (and try only to ask questions that you don't mind being asked back):

1) If name tag indicates person's job: *I see you (fill in blank). What's it like to (fill in blank with something benign about the job they do)?* For example: *I see you do media relations for the union. What's it like to talk with reporters about education?*

2) If name tag doesn't indicate person's job: *What kind of work do you do?* or *How are you connected with this event?*

3) *How did you end up doing the job you're doing now?*

4) *What do you like best about what you do?* (Or, alternately: *What's the most challenging part of what you do?*)

5) *Is there a certain aspect of education you're most interested in?*

6) *How are you enjoying (the city you are in or conference you're at)?*

time you're asked the question, you've had time to think about it, and are ready with a good answer. The third time you're asked that exact question, you can answer confidently and with the flair of a seasoned professional.

Below are five questions that you should always be ready for. People will ask you these questions at school, conferences, dinners and even at the park while you're pushing your child on the swing (trust me, I've been there). Consider yourself warned!

Have a 30-second to one-minute answer that you've thought out in advance. You don't have to answer exactly the same way every time, and what you will notice is that your answers will evolve over time.

1) So, what's it like to be Teacher of the Year?

2) How did you become Teacher of the Year?

3) What sets you apart from other teachers?

4) *Version 1*: What types of things have you done as Teacher of the Year?
   Version 2: What types of things do you hope to do as Teacher of the Year?

5) What's been the best part of being Teacher of the Year?

If you are part of a group that consists of other TOYs, be sure to pay attention to how they answer these questions. You can formulate some fantastic answers by listening to those given by your colleagues!

My Advice: *Be a Superstar!* When people ask you about being a Teacher of the Year, they are genuinely interested, so give them an answer that is honest, and will leave them laughing, crying, reflecting or moved to action!

TACKLING TABLES FOR TEN

Most education conference and Teacher of the Year award dinners all utilize the same type of seating arrangements: large, round tables that seat ten people. These tables allow the servers to serve (usually pre-selected food options) and clear quickly, while moving around the room in an efficient manner. For those of us sitting at the tables, it can be a challenge to navigate and carry on conversations.

How can you carry on a conversation with ten people across a huge table? *You can't.* Perhaps the table can engage for a minute or so, but the conversation will quickly be fragmented into smaller conversations. Don't fear, though, I have a solution for you!

 ## THE KAJITANI TRIANGLE

A good, realistic strategy for carrying on effective conversations at large tables is what I like to call "The Kajitani Triangle." In short, think in "triangles," and set your goal to have a conversation with no more than two others at the same time (with yourself as the third point on the triangle). For example:

You are person #1, and you focus on carrying on a conversation with the person to your left (# 10) and to your right (#2).

You are person #1, and you focus on carrying on a conversation with the two people to your left (#9 and #10) or the two people to your right (#2 and #3).

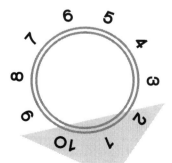

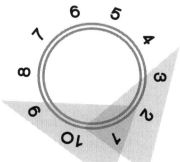

If there is someone sitting outside of your triangle that you really want to meet, touch base with them after the meal, or during a break. Don't break The Kajitani Triangle! (I know it's a bit "obtuse," but it works!) Letting go of trying to make the awkward reach beyond your triangles at the dinner can help you relax and digest much better.

Most often, you will end up simply talking to only the person to your immediate left or right. Ask questions, tell stories, and have fun!

TOY TALK ...

"My advice would be to make the most of every moment and every interaction. Now that you have the big title of TOY next to your name, people will seek your opinion and ideas. Speak from your heart about what you are passionate about and share your love for teaching with those who will listen. You never know what new opportunities will open up for you.

I found myself having an in-depth conversation with the State Superintendent. I was honest and spoke from my heart, and the next thing I knew, I was invited to help make positive change in California as a member of the Education Technology Task Force.

This is your chance to share with a large audience how dedicated, determined, and innovative educators are. You represent us all!"

Jo-Ann Fox, *San Diego County Teacher of the Year*

CHaPTeR 8

THe SPOTLIGHT IS On: HanDLInG THe meDia

Kind of like cocktail parties, being a media subject may be one of those things you never thought — or never wished — to do when you became a teacher. Or maybe you're itching for the opportunity to get your important message out to the media and the world. Either way, now that you're a Teacher of the Year, handling your role as a media subject has become part of your job.

I'll tell you this: if you're media wary and you want to grudgingly do one or two interviews with the local reporter who calls, then hide from any press thereafter, you can. I've seen TOYs do that. Yet, as you may be getting used to me saying by now — that sure would be a waste of a great opportunity for you to speak up for teachers, students and whatever educational issues you are passionate about.

As a TOY, you have the chance to present a positive image of educators to a huge audience, via the media. Whether we love or hate "the media," we cannot deny that it has power — the power to reach many people, and to influence many people.

I say, rather than let the media fall only into the hands of the dark forces of commercialism (that we deal with in our students each day), let's take a piece of that influence into our own hands, and make a positive difference for education!

GETTING POSITIVE PRESS COVERAGE

So, the first step of handling media is getting media coverage. This, in itself, is of course the subject of many a book and undergraduate degree. So, again, here I'm going to cover the basics I've learned as a TOY to help you get your message into the hands of the press.

First, it's important to know a little secret that I and other TOYs have discovered: *the media love a good education story!* You know that little spot at the end of the evening news, where they plug in something uplifting or inspiring each night? Yep, they are looking for people just like us to fill that spot!

ALEX'S STORY

HOW I LANDED ON THE CBS EVENING NEWS WITH KATIE COURIC

One day during my TOY year, I got an email from a producer from the *CBS Evening News with Katie Couric* who was looking to do a story on an algebra initiative in California. The producer had seen a news story from our local CBS affiliate station about me and my alter ego, "The Rappin' Mathematician," teaching algebra through rap songs that I write and produce, so she contacted me.

We made a phone date, and after we had talked about the algebra initiative a bit, she asked me about my personal story of becoming "The Rappin' Mathematician." I knew this was my chance, so I launched enthusiastically into my story (which I had practiced and knew how to deliver in a succinct, compelling way!).

(continued on next page)

56

ALEX'S STORY *(continued)*

Sure enough, she was so taken with the story, she decided she wanted to do a feature just on me instead. She made arrangements with my district superintendent, and I soon had the surreal experience of a *CBS Evening News* crew coming to my classroom.

When the story ran, I had to pinch myself, as they not only made me look good as a teacher, they even included a shot of both of my CDs (available at www.mathraps.com, by the way!) — and Katie Couric ended the story by saying, "I love that guy!" I couldn't believe my good fortune. My CD sales were better in the two months following that news segment than in the three years prior, combined! (And in all the time since, combined!) People still mention the story to this day.

Of course, even though the producer was the one who approached me, the real backstory of this story is all the hustling I did up to that point — to create my CDs while also teaching full-time (with a new baby), to get them into people's hands, to get onto the local CBS affiliate station in the first place. As writer Diana Rankin said, "It takes 20 years of hard work to become an overnight sensation."

So, if you're a TOY who is generating some buzz, members of the media may just come knocking at your door. But, that may not be the case for you at the moment (and, by the way, it was for me only for a moment; now I usually do the door-knocking!). That said, how can we be proactive about getting a story into the media? There are two basic ways: press releases and developing direct relationships with members of the media.

1) Press Releases

If you are contacted by a reporter who is interested in doing a story about you, it's likely that they learned about you from a press release that someone else wrote (your school or district, your county office of education, or the organization that selected you). These days, individuals also write press releases. It's a basic announcement sent to the media about a story idea — if you search it online, you will find many samples and the simple format (though there is an art to a good press release — as always, great writing and creativity open doors!).

Check into whether the organization that selected you sent out a press release. If so, contact the person who wrote it (usually a public relations or media relations staff member) and suggest additional places to send it, such as your alma mater or professional association magazines or websites. Or, ask for a copy to send it out yourself as well.

If approached with kindness and respect, most "PR people" at the organizations we work with as TOYs are happy to work with you to get your story out — in the long run, it makes them look better if you get more media coverage. TOY press releases will generally go to education reporters at any news outlet, as well as education-centered media outlets.

2) Developing a Direct Relationship with Members of the Media

This is not as intimidating as it sounds. As I've learned from my wife, who was a newspaper journalist before she went into academia, it's part of reporters' jobs to develop relationships with potential story leads and quotable experts. As a TOY and a recognized teacher-leader, you are a great story lead and quotable expert for an education reporter!

So, find out who the education reporters are for your local newspapers, radio and TV news stations, and drop them a note to introduce yourself and to offer a story suggestion (see suggested wording and expert advice on the next page). I've found that when I'm sincere about the work I'm doing — and keep my focus on the work, rather than on me — reporters have been friendly and responsive.

You can also do this with reporters from different magazines related to education and your platform or cause. Then, whenever you, your school or organization are involved in something you feel could be newsworthy, let your media contacts know what's happening!

By the way, it's easy to make your own newsworthy stories by inviting (or having students invite) high-profile visitors such as politicians, sports stars, artists, or other inspiring trailblazers to your school to speak to your students, as part of your lessons (which many of us TOYs did well before we were TOYs!). But, now, invite your media contacts to cover these visits, so you continue to feed positive stories about education into the news.

Once you begin to think about what makes a good media story, it's amazing how natural it becomes to generate them. My wife, Megan, also reminds me that as a newspaper reporter she had to come up with at least 10 stories a week, so she always appreciated a nice story being handed to her — remember this if you think reporters don't want to hear from you!

SAMPLE EMAIL OF INTRODUCTION TO A REPORTER

To: Jamie Diaz

From: Alex Kajitani

Subject: Story Idea from California Teacher of the Year

Dear Ms. Diaz:

I'm the current California Teacher of the Year, and I wanted to drop you a line to introduce myself. I greatly appreciate your recent stories on the rising high school dropout rates in our county, an issue I'm also deeply concerned about.

I thought you might be interested in covering a project I'm doing with my middle school math students, in which they're studying real statistics on salaries, home ownership and other outcomes for people with and without high school, college, or other higher education degrees. It has, of course, turned out to be not just a math lesson for them, but a life one.

Please let me know if you'd like to visit my classroom and check it out, or if I can be a resource for any other education stories.

Best,

Alex Kajitani
California Teacher of the Year
www.AlexKajitani.com

SHINING ON CAMERA

Once the opportunity for media coverage arises, you want to be prepared. This is especially true when the media coverage involves being on camera. Though I've been interviewed on camera now many times, it still brings me that zing of nervous excitement when the camera crew shows up.

ALEX KAJITANI'S TOP TEN TIPS FOR CAMERA-READY TOYS

Here are 10 Tips I've learned to ensure that you look and sound like the superstar that you are:

1) **Less is more.** Keep your wardrobe simple! Avoid clothing with lots of patterns or intricate designs. This keeps the viewers' focus on your face and your message. Solid, middle-tone clothing colors come off best on camera. Also, with the increased use of green screen technology these days, it's a good bet to leave the green at home.

   ✓ Men: Ties with intricate patterns can be distracting, or can appear a bit blurry on camera. Also, white shirts (with no jacket) are difficult to capture well on camera.

   ✓ Women: Avoid jewelry that dangles, jangles or swings, which can clink on lapel microphones. Jewelry that is is too flashy can also reflect light, causing further distraction. Also, you may want to bring your own makeup, to avoid being "powdered up" in the wrong color tones for you.

2) **Match your wardrobe and your message.** Too often, I see teachers on camera talking about how teachers should be treated like professionals, and yet look like they're dressed for a hike in their local mountains. Unless you're a science teacher actually giving an interview in the mountains (and really, maybe even then), please consider wearing truly professional-looking attire for media appearances.

   If we want to be paid and respected as professionals in society, we can do our part to show them that we *are* professionals. I'm not saying a business suit is required for every show; but take the time to make sure you look like the experienced expert you are — credible, comfortable and confident.

3) **Do your homework.** If you know you're going to be on the local news in a few days, take time to watch it, and become familiar with what it looks like to the viewer. Ask yourself: *How are the news anchors who sit behind the desk dressed? What about the reporters who are out in the field? What are the other guests wearing? What's the tone of the show?*

   It's worth asking the reporter or host when you agree to appear what kind of topics or questions to expect. But, even if they give you an answer, be prepared for anything; they may or may not stick to it!

4) **Coordinate when possible.** Once, I showed up to do an on-camera interview with the four other TOYs from our county. We consisted of a group of three men, and two women. As luck would have it, all three men were wearing tan jackets with a blue shirt underneath. What we each perceived to be our individual styles ended up looking like we were wearing a uniform.

   If you know you are going to be filmed with others, try in advance to discuss what you'll be wearing. This also avoids some of the men wearing ties while others aren't, or some of the women wearing cocktail dresses and one wearing jeans (again, please, go at least with business casual when in the media!). If you do not have an opportunity to coordinate in advance, bring a change of clothes, just in case you end up wearing the same thing as someone else being filmed with you.

5) **Expect the heat.** Camera lights are HOT. If they make you perspire easily, try to have some water just out of the camera's frame, keep a handkerchief or tissue in your pocket, and dress in clothing that is light, or in layers. (It's also smart to have a mini-deodorant in your purse or car!)

6) **ALWAYS, always ask for a copy** of the video or segment once you're finished. Be sure to watch it, share it, and send the producer a thank you note! (Remember, this also helps seal your connection for the next time you're looking for media coverage.) Through social media outlets, you can give people advance notice of when and where you'll be appearing and what you'll be talking about. Once it's over, you can share the footage for the entire world to see!

7) **Smile!** Nothing will make you look or "sound" better than a smile on your face. Just a small, natural smile will do.

8) **Speak in soundbytes.** Keeping your answers short and simple is the key to sounding great on camera (or on the radio). In this modern age of quick transitions, soundbytes and visual effects, talking for too long actually makes you appear *less* credible.

Always have some of your favorite one-liners ready to roll off your lips. Take your best stories, and work to shorten them to only the most essential parts, so you can tell them quickly, in a way that is memorable. (Notice this repeating theme about your stories.) Often, newspaper/magazine reporters will ask if they can record your interview, and will pick-and-choose their quotes later.

Remember: *EVERYTHING you say is "on the record." If you don't want it broadcast or printed, don't say it.*

TOY TALK ...

"When fishing for a soundbyte, sometimes reporters will let you stumble around after you finish your answer, hoping you'll say something interesting, or stupid. When you're done with your answer (and do try to be done earlier rather than later!), just smile and wait. They'll edit it down later."

Michael Geisen, *National Teacher of the Year*

9) **Connect.** If possible, get to know the person who will be interviewing you on camera before the cameras are rolling (even if it means introducing yourself during a commercial break).

Even the smallest bit of connection in advance will help you feel more comfortable with the interviewer, and the more comfortable you are, the more you will shine!

10) **Be real.** When you speak, the goal is to be confident and articulate, but not every word you utter will be beautiful and profound. Be the person that you are: authentic, real and realistic.

If you mess up, smile, and keep going. You have nothing to prove, just something to share. And remember, just the fact that you are in the news makes you an instant star to the students you serve!

FIT TO PRINT

Much of the advice for on-camera or on-radio interviews also applies to interviews with print reporters: make a connection, be real, do your homework, smile, be professional. Even some of the clothing advice applies, because often a print reporter will bring a still photographer with them to take a photo of you in your classroom or school site.

The other advice that also applies to print that I want to reiterate, and reiterate — and, one more time, reiterate:

1) <u>**EVERYTHING**</u> **you say is "on the record."** If you don't want it broadcast or printed, don't say it. Not even that little joke that just might be off-color for some. Not even that tiny dig about the infamously stingy superintendent. Do. Not. Say. It.

2) **Be as *clear* and *succinct* as possible.** Truth is, with print stories, exactly what comes out of your mouth is rarely exactly what ends up in the paper. Most print reporters don't have time to tape record and transcribe interviews word-for-word — they usually write from the notes they are subtly but furiously typing or scribbling as you're talking to them. And, they need to somehow craft your conversation into a compelling story.

   That said, to give yourself the best shot at having your quotes be as close as possible to what you actually said: be very clear on your message, and convey it through great stories and succinct statements.

This all takes some practice, so forgive yourself if it doesn't go perfectly the first (or fifteenth) time you give a media interview, but keep working on it — there is a reason people study this and get paid to train others on it. It's as much of an art to give a great interview as it is to conduct one.

EXPERT ADVICE...

FOCUS ON WHAT YOU DO

"When you approach reporters for publicity about being named a Teacher of the Year, you're likely to get different responses depending on the reporter and the publication. Some, especially those who cover the school district where you work, will jump at the chance. Others may take more convincing.

In either case, make it easy on the reporter by focusing on what it is about your teaching style that earned you the recognition. Show some humility about the recognition so you don't come off as somebody seeking publicity for self-promotion. That just may backfire and you'll end up with little or no publicity.

Take the focus off yourself. One approach is to say something about being honored by the recognition, but also excited because it gives you an opportunity to talk about a classroom technique you want other teachers to know about. This is a chance to share whatever techniques, strategies or innovations you have.

Tell the reporter not just about yourself, but about what you do. Have some anecdotes to tell to illustrate your message. If possible, find a former student or parent who can tell about how your technique made a difference with them.

(continued on next page)

EXPERT ADVICE *(continued)*...

A story about a Teacher of the Year that only talks about the person's biography is not going to be read by many people. A story that tells people about something new in education that seems to be working is going to be read, remembered and passed around by parents, politicians and even other teachers."

Gary Warth, *long-time newspaper reporter and current education reporter for the San Diego Union-Tribune*

BE THE MEDIA

If you enjoy writing or making video or audio recordings, another way to get media coverage is to create it yourself!

Op-eds (newspapers' guest editorials) and letters to the editor are great ways to get your message published; I've written two op-eds for regional newspapers on education issues, both co-authored with another teacher-leader. There are first-person essays published in major magazines like *Newsweek*.

And of course the sky's the limit with writing or creating videos for online media. Think *Huffington Post, Examiner.com,* AOL's *Patch* — all seeking experts like TOYs to write blog columns that are circulated widely.

We'll talk more about that in the Social Media chapter. But do keep in mind that a free media is part of democracy, and these days you are more free than ever to create media, as well as be a subject of it!

TOY TALK ...

"As a TOY, you will be asked countless questions because you are now considered an 'educational expert' by the virtue of your award. Some questions may be more difficult to answer than others.

When faced with those tough questions, remember to speak of what you know best — your classroom. You are the educational expert who drives your students, and you can answer any question when you frame it from your standpoint as a classroom teacher."

Stephanie Doyle, *Virginia Teacher of the Year*

CHAPTER 9

TEACHING TEACHERS: CONFERENCE PRESENTATIONS

I love education conferences. Truly. I enjoy getting out of the classroom for a day or two, listening to keynote speakers, sitting in on breakout sessions, and meeting other educators. I usually return to the classroom with a fresh perspective, great ideas and renewed energy.

Among the opportunities that arose when I was named a TOY were invitations to present at conferences. When a Teacher of the Year presents at a conference, it's a win for all involved. As a TOY, you get an audience to present your best ideas. Audience members return to their classrooms with your enlightened perspective, and/ or excited to try out some of the strategies you're presenting. It also reflects well on the organization holding the conference, as having a TOY as a presenter shows their ability to provide conference attendees access to the top teachers and ideas.

HOW TO PRESENT AT A CONFERENCE

There are two steps to great conference presentations: preparing before a conference, and presenting at the conference. There are a few simple strategies I've learned about both steps that can help you make the most of education conferences as a TOY.

BEFORE THE CONFERENCE:

1) **Pick your topic.** Decide what you would like to present on. If you're having trouble deciding, ask yourself the following questions:

   ✓ What am I most passionate about in education (i.e., your platform)?

   ✓ What do I do well in my own classroom that other teachers would benefit from?

   ✓ What have other teachers consistently asked me to share with them over the years?

2) **Write your blurb.** Once you've identified your topic, turn it into a workshop by selecting a title, and a 200-word description of your workshop. Some conferences will require a description with less words; you can modify as necessary. (See my example at the end of this chapter.) Picking a catchy title always helps bring attention and audience members to your workshop.

3) **Make your pitch.** If you haven't been invited to present already, find a conference at which you would like to present (I highly recommend starting with a local conference in your area), and find out how to submit a presentation proposal (sometimes called an RFP, "Request for Proposal," or an abstract). Each conference has a committee that selects presenters, and usually has a window of time in which you can submit your proposal.

   If you really want to present at a particular conference, but have missed the deadline, it's always worth contacting the conference organizer(s) and seeing if you can still submit. As a math teacher, conference organizers usually receive less applications to present in the area of math, and are happy to extend the deadline in order to get more "math people" on board! If they will not extend the deadline, don't fret. Thank them for their time, and let them know how excited you are about applying for next year.

4) **Be easy.** If you are notified that your proposal has been accepted, be sure to get all information the conference organizers request from you to them in a timely, organized and friendly manner. Remember: conference organizers are extremely busy, and often overwhelmed. Showing them that you are easy to work with will solidify your reputation as a professional, and often result in being invited to return in the future.

AT THE CONFERENCE:

1) **Be prepared and flexible.** Be sure to determine and communicate what equipment you will need to deliver a smashing presentation. Sometimes, projectors, screens and chart paper will be provided. Sometimes, they will not!

There are times when I show up, connect my laptop, and begin presenting. There are other times when I have to haul in my own projector, speakers, handouts, etc. Every conference is different, so know in advance what will (and will not) be provided, and make sure you are prepared for it to work or not work! (Yes, this means always having a low-tech backup plan.)

2) **Go early.** Get to the conference with plenty of time to spare. Whenever possible, I like to take a peek at the room I'll be presenting in, just to begin to envision the physical surroundings. If there is another presenter in the room at the time, I try to listen to them for a bit, noticing things like lighting, acoustics, and seating arrangements.

3) **Learn by doing.** Pay attention during your presentation. What is going well? What needs to be improved? Was your joke a good one? The first conference presentation I ever gave, "Making Math Cool," is one that I still give today. However, each time I present it, I notice something I could be doing better, make adjustments here and there, or try something new. These days, that presentation is *a lot* better than when I first gave it!

4) **Connect the dots.** If there's a conference keynote or very popular speaker sometime before your presentation, it's always great to go, get inspired (hopefully!), and then reference a point or two from that in your presentation. Any way you can integrate ideas circulating at the conference into your presentation can help your audience connect the dots, and it will make your presentation feel "fresher," of-the-moment, and wholly relevant to the conference conversation.

5) **Have fun.** While you're at the conference, soak it in and enjoy it. Sit in on other presentations, introduce yourself to the people sitting next to you, and eat lunch with people you've never met before. Visit the exhibitors' booths and share what you learn with your colleagues back at school!

REAL CONFERENCE WORKSHOP EXTRACT EXAMPLE 1

One of the conference workshops of **Angie Miller,** *New Hampshire Teacher of the Year:*

Writing Will Save The World (or at Least Your Classroom): Common Core Writing in the Content Area Classroom

The new Common Core Standards require content area teachers to teach writing in their classrooms, yet most content area teachers do not feel prepared to teach writing and are overwhelmed by the idea of implementing writing in their curriculum. In a lively and approachable way, Angie Miller, the 2011 New Hampshire Teacher of the Year and a TED speaker, will address the real concerns that content teachers have about teaching writing: implementation, evaluation, and methodology.

In the end, participants will recognize that writing is an exciting way to increase student achievement and engagement and walk away with immediate tools to use in the classroom.

ReaL COnFeRenCe WORKSHOP exTRaCT exaMPLe II

One of my conference workshops:

Making Math Cool

Let's be honest: you can't teach math if your students are bored, unengaged or struggling with the basics. Join Alex Kajitani, California Teacher of the Year, for a bold and honest look at traditional mathematics education, and what to do about it.

Participants will leave with creative, easy-to-implement strategies and activities that will ignite your math lessons the very next day. Create a classroom culture where students understand the real-world relevance of mathematics and say, "Hey, that's pretty cool — and so is my teacher!"

CHAPTER 10

THE REST OF THE TEAM: COLLEAGUE RELATIONSHIPS

There are a lot of great things about becoming a Teacher of the Year, and colleague relationships can be one of them. Let's give a big cheer right now for the wonderful colleagues at our school sites and districts who are endless sources of encouragement and support for us. (Hip hip hooray, and thank you very much!)

However, here's where I also must reveal the first truth about the shadow side of being named a TOY. It's really important to know and be prepared for. Are you ready?

NOT EVERYONE WILL SUPPORT YOUR SUCCESS

Yep, not everyone will support your success. It's a bummer, but it's true. Not everyone is going to be on your cheering squad, and sometimes the attention on you can bring out the worst in people around you. At times, it will be your colleagues; other times it may be your friends, family or even strangers. We live in a society that is obsessed with stardom and success, with a dark edge, and distorted attitudes that may start in Hollywood can permeate into our everyday, human interactions.

Let's focus on colleagues here. For whatever reason, all of a sudden you're a Teacher of the Year, and are getting accolades left and right. Because your colleagues know your strengths and weaknesses so well from working with you every day, they know that often, what a newspaper article says about you doesn't cover the "whole truth." They also know how hard *they* work, just like you. So, the first celebration for you might have your colleagues excited and supportive; however, by the third cake, can't we see how they might get a little bit sick of it?

While we are supposed to constantly celebrate the success of our students, constantly celebrating the success of a single colleague (especially when everyone is equally working hard) can get tiring and difficult. Some teachers may think that it should have been them selected instead of you.

A TOY friend of mine once told me that whenever his teaching team came up against a difficult decision, one of his colleagues would blurt out, "Well, let's ask Bill — he's the *Teacher of the Year*."

Another TOY told me that when the selection committee came to observe her teaching, another teacher at her site stopped a member of the committee and said, "You know, she's just going to put on a dog-and-pony show for you today. She's not really that good of a teacher."

Obviously, in the above two scenarios, as well as in countless others that play themselves out with TOYs, the unsupportive colleagues' problems were not just limited to the situation at hand. They had built-up resentment, and were now expressing it in a way that was unproductive for the teachers and students.

SIX STRATEGIES TO UN-GRUDGE GRUDGING COLLEAGUES

While you can't control every person's emotions or handle every situation perfectly, there are a few things you can do to minimize the times when colleagues may feel the urge to be unsupportive:

1) **Express gratitude.** Be sure to thank as many people as possible for helping you to be successful. Communicate effectively that the reason you were named Teacher of the Year is the fantastic support you have received from those you work with. It's true: we could never have done it alone.

2) **Walk in their shoes.** It's always helpful to imagine how those grumbling colleagues are feeling. Let's face it, we all know teacher morale isn't at an all-time high these days, with budget cuts everywhere we turn. So, these colleagues may feel overworked, underpaid, underappreciated, and downright scared.

   A scarcity mentality often develops in times like these, where people feel they are fighting for their jobs and there aren't enough to go around. So, goes that line of thinking, *if my colleague is getting all the the good stuff, that doesn't leave any for me.* Remembering this (though not believing it) can help you empathize with your naysayers, and not take their jabs personally.

3) **Be upfront, and deal with it.** If you sense hostility — or if it's outright — it may be time to simply call out the elephant in the room. Sometimes just naming the beast — "I know, I am getting a ridiculous amount of attention lately!" — can diffuse tensions.

   If it's one colleague, try to find a time to talk to that person alone, in a direct but positive manner, asking how you can make the situation easier for them. If it is within your staff group, consider saying something to them all at a meeting or meal. (See in a moment how the Alaska Teacher of the Year handled this — also using another great strategy: *humor!*)

4) **Minimize talk of the glamorous parts of being a TOY.** In other words, don't fan the flames of resentment by dousing them with stories about the fancy dinners you were invited

to or the important people you've met. It's great to share with your close family and friends, but with colleagues, it seems that most TOYs have found it better to be selective in how and when they talk about their TOY events.

One of my TOY friends advises that there's one thing *NOT* to say to your colleagues after a TOY event: *"Oh my gosh, you wouldn't believe the quality of the people I met! These are the most talented, creative and dedicated teachers I've met in my entire time teaching!"* (As Homer Simpson would say: "D-oh!!")

This advice also may apply to your social media posts — some TOYs have found it wiser to curb the amount of "TOY talk" on their personal social media pages, where they are often "friends" with IRL (in real life) teaching colleagues. Instead, they save the glamorous TOY photos for their blogs or separate, professional social media pages, where people are there because they want to hear about it.

It's a fine line between being humble and cagey, and we each have to find the most authentic way for us to handle discussions with colleagues. But, as a general rule, I recommend leaving most of the TOY Talk for fellow TOYs and your own support circle, or your professional circle online — and minimizing it when with your everyday teaching colleagues.

5) **Make an effort to help, socialize, collaborate and still be "one of the gang."** It's the small gestures that colleagues appreciate. When you stick around to stack chairs after the assembly, when you show up in the teacher's lounge to have lunch with them, when you nominate them for a grant that came across your desk, or offer them your companion ticket to a movie screening. Stop and pick up trash in the hallways. Ask your colleagues for help, with technology or whatever expertise they have that you've always valued (including new teachers, who bring in new skills and perspectives).

No need to go overboard "proving yourself" to still be you, but it does help to remember that the small gestures as a colleague matter — and are amplified when all eyes are peeled on you, wondering if you're "too cool for school."

6) **Ignore it.** Sometimes, whatever you do, someone is going to have it out for you. In that case, just stay focused on what you need to do in order to be the best teacher-leader you can.

Remember that the negative feelings that others express usually have very little to do with you. Don't let them stand in the way of the incredible work you are doing, and the potential to use your TOY status to better the lives of your students, and the others whose lives you touch.

BOB WILLIAMS' STORY

a Great example of Keeping Colleagues on Your Team

When Bob Williams was named Alaska's Teacher of the Year, he flew out to Texas to meet with the other TOYs from each state — called the STOY group. While there, he heard many stories about how fellow STOYs were dealing with unsupportive, and at times even nasty, colleagues. The idea of damaging collegiality with his staff because of his STOY award frightened Bob.

So, when he returned from Texas, he stood up at this next staff meeting, and said:

(continued on next page)

BOB WILLIAMS' STORY *(continued)*

"Hey, some TOYs from other states won a brand new car or $10,000, and their colleagues in their schools are jealous and resent them. I did not win any money with this award, unless you count the value of the plaque and a piece of cake. I value your friendship, but I have to tell you: I would definitely trade it in a heartbeat for $10,000 or a new car. However, I did not get $10,000 or a new car, so I would be devastated if I lost your friendship for a piece of cake."

His colleagues, cracked up, and his TOY experience ultimately strengthened his friendships with them.

Of course, some of your everyday colleagues will be just great about your award, from the get-go, and they'll make the whole experience all the sweeter. I only tell you about the grudging colleagues because it's something I've seen nearly every TOY I know deal with, and I wish I'd known myself before it happened, so I could have been prepared with a graceful strategy or two to handle it. Thus, the strategies I just offered you here.

TOY TALK ...

"I have one point to share with any new Teacher of the Year: To maintain the cheers you receive from the learning community, you need to maintain the vigor that made you a TOY, keeping your priority always for teaching. The real joy lies in helping our students, using our efficiency and effectiveness as the best teachers!"

Murali Gopal, *American Samoa Teacher of the Year*

OUTSIDE OF SCHOOL: YOUR NEW TOY COLLEAGUES

When you are chosen as a Teacher of the Year, you also get a whole new circle of colleagues: fellow TOYs! Especially if you are a member of a group of TOYs chosen for your state, county, district or organization, it's likely you will get to meet these fellow motivated, innovative teachers at events surrounding the award. While it may seem hard to connect and keep in touch with those fellow TOYs, I highly recommend you make the effort, exchange information, and follow up.

Fellow TOYs can be like gold as you navigate your newly heightened role as a teacher-leader, as they are traveling the path with you — or have traveled it before you! These are the people you can really talk details about your TOY adventure with, rather than your school colleagues (who simply have another — important, but different — role in your life now). You may have certain aspirations and approaches more in common with a fellow TOY from another state than you have with a fellow teacher at your own school.

A NATURAL CONNECTION

This is only natural, and happens with sub-groups and leaders in any profession. When my wife, Megan, was a career counselor at the University of California, she was part of a sub-group of counselors from different research universities who specialized in working with doctoral students. She found herself looking forward to that group's annual meeting as the professional highlight of her year, and often emailed and collaborated with those colleagues outside of her university even more than the colleagues within her own career center.

It's not that she didn't like or value her in-house colleagues, just that she had something specific in common with this specialized group of colleagues who were spread across the continent, just one of them in each research university. There were issues they could relate better with each other, targeted information and opportunities they could share — and they felt less isolated in their work by being connected with one another.

I've found this to also be true for me with the fellow TOYs — and other like-minded teacher-leaders — I've met from all different places. I just relate more to my TOY colleagues than my school colleagues in certain ways, and I feel less isolated and more motivated to keep stretching beyond my classroom by knowing them. Many have shared with me that they feel the same.

TOY TALK ...

"Receiving the Milken National Educator Award was amazing because it was not just about what I had done, but an acknowledgment of what the Milken Family Foundation knew I would accomplish in the future. Having a network of people who believe in you and your ability to make a difference in education is extremely powerful!"

Shannon Garrison, *Milken National Educator*

I can't express how much my collaborations and friendships with fellow TOYs have meant to me as I move into the next stage of my career in education. Being a TOY has also allowed me the opportunity to connect with other high-profile teacher-leaders throughout the country. I'm now partnering with other TOYs and teacher-leaders from all over on major projects, and they are often the ones I call when I need to process a new or challenging situation.

So, while you continue to nurture your relationships with your everyday colleagues, I also encourage you to take advantage of the new colleagues you've now inherited — other TOYs and teacher-leaders who have been offered the spotlight to make a bigger impact on education, like you have!

TOY TALK ...

"The first time our group of State Teachers of the Year met in Dallas, I remember thinking that I was so lucky to find people who shared my enthusiasm and passion for teaching, and that I was not alone. Embrace and cherish the friendships with fellow TOYs that will develop and last beyond that year."

Alice King, *Wyoming Teacher of the Year*

CHAPTER 11

TOYS ONLINE:
USING BLOGS & SOCIAL MEDIA AS A TOY

Teachers of the Year have been named by schools since, well, probably the beginning of formal education. (Our country's State and National Teacher of the Year Program has been around since 1952. And countless organizations have also been naming Teachers of the Year throughout the past century.)

The internet, however, has only been readily available to the last decade of TOYs. But, what a difference it can make!

The internet offers unlimited opportunity for us, as TOYs, to spread our messages more broadly and reach more people. Of course, there are downsides to our culture's internet obsession (can you say short attention spans?), but let's focus on making the web work for our positive impact as Teachers of the Year.

Blogs, Facebook, Twitter, Pinterest, Instagram... These are the top social media outlets at the time I'm writing this book. Speculation abounds over which of these will survive and which will be tomorrow's *Jeopardy* question. So, rather than focus on these specific social media outlets, I'd like to focus this chapter on offering general tips for most effectively using social media as a TOY.

Basically, I've seen three ways that TOYs use social media to make a positive impact on education: chronicling their journey, spreading their message, and creating an image. Let's dive a bit into each.

CHRONICLING YOUR JOURNEY

Launching a blog (short for "weblog") when you're selected as a Teacher of the Year is a great idea for two main reasons:

1) It lets you keep a working document that chronicles all the great, inspiring, and challenging experiences of your year in the spotlight.

2) It lets other people follow your journey — both making it easier for you to keep people in the loop (sending them to one central place) and allowing you to begin to build an audience for your platform.

TOY TALK ...

"My advice is that, as a Teacher of the Year, you document your experiences throughout the year by blogging or journaling. A blog is the 21st Century version of a diary, and I am so glad I captured my year in pictures and descriptive narratives of every school I visited, every pre-service teacher I met, every education policy meeting I attended, and every reflection I wrote about teaching.

It was a personal growth experience for me, but it also gave me the opportunity to share with teachers, friends, and family members who were able to keep up with my Teacher of the Year adventures."

Cindi Rigsbee, *North Carolina Teacher of the Year*

If you decide to launch your own blog, it's free and easy on sites such as WordPress and Blogger (again, these are today's hot platforms, and others may come onto the scene). You can give your blog a clever title, and choose a design template and color scheme that fit your style. It's simple to post photos, videos, links and reflections, and you can even print the whole thing out at the end of your year as a souvenir book on sites like Blog2Print, Blurb and others.

Cindi Rigsbee, North Carolina TOY, created her personal chronicle blog on Blogger, which you can see here: http://thedreamteacher. blogspot.com.

To build your blog audience, try these strategies:

1) Begin by sending an email to all of your contacts, personal and professional, about your blog. Encourage them to sign up for updates on your posts via a blog feed, or your email newsletter list.

2) Announce the start of your blog on your social media accounts (Facebook, Twitter, etc.).

3) List your blog URL in your email signature (under your Teacher of the Year title), so anyone you correspond with can click on it.

4) Comment on other education blogs by signing in through your blog platform — then anyone who reads your comments can click on your blog as well.

GREAT EXAMPLE OF A CHRONICLE BLOG

Tony Mullen: *Road Diaries: 2009 Teacher of the Year*
http://blogs.edweek.org/teachers/teacher_of_the_year/

(continued on next page)

GREAT EXAMPLE OF A CHRONICLE BLOG *(continued)*

Beautifully written, the blog of Tony Mullen, the 2009 National Teacher of the Year (and a former New York City police officer-turned alternative high school teacher in Connecticut) is about his journeys as the country's 59th National Teacher of the Year. His blog, like his travels, is a collection of esoteric thoughts and observations written for and about teachers.

Tony calls it like he sees it, often expressing frustration with a system that does little to support teachers in reality. In his blog entries, he often puts into words the universal feelings of all teachers. According to Tony, teachers are the fulcrum that supports this whole enterprise we call education, and people should be aware that any movement in that fulcrum affects us all.

(Note that Tony's blog is on *EdWeek*. As the National Teacher of the Year, his chronicle of his year traveling the nation and representing all teachers was a desirable blog for them. For the rest of us, chronicle blogs will mostly be launched on our own, and sites like *EdWeek* are more likely to be interested in "message" or issue-based blogs, as we'll discuss next.)

SPREADING YOUR MESSAGE

While a personal blog is a great way to chronicle your TOY journey, there are other places you can blog online if you really want to spread the broader message of your education platform niche. *The Huffington Post*, AOL's *Patch*, and *Examiner.com* are well-read sites that readily accept bloggers like Teachers of the

Year who have something significant they want to write about. You can also check with education sites, such as *Edutopia* and *EdWeek*, about blogging for them.

To apply as a blogger for these kinds of sites, the protocol is usually to send a direct email to the relevant editor, introducing yourself and what you want to blog about (your platform, issue or message in education). They usually don't pay, but they allow you to get much more exposure than a personal blog, if you want to get people talking about the issue you're passionate about, or to build your reputation to do more work in your field.

Megan (my wife and co-author) blogs for both *Huffington Post* and AOL's *Patch*. As an example, one of her education-related blog posts on *Huffington Post* (about California's education budget crisis) got 588 "likes" and 343 comments. That's a pretty good number of people reading her message and talking about it.

She notes for new public bloggers that *Huffington Post* comments tend to be more harsh than *Patch* or *Examiner* comments — though more people read *Huffington Post*. You can choose whether or not to engage in the comments (for the controversial article above, Megan chose not to engage with angry, anonymous commenters, but she usually does engage with the friendlier commenters on *Patch*). On this note, putting yourself out there as a public blogger on education issues can elicit some intense debate, so be ready for it — and remember to try not to take it personally!

Whenever one of your public blog posts runs, be sure to spread the word on social media to let people know to read it right away. It always helps to ask them to "like" it on the site (if they like it!) and to comment, as the more "likes" and comments you get, the more prominently and longer your post will be displayed on the site.

You can also start a platform or message blog yourself, using the same kind of blog host sites mentioned earlier (WordPress, Blogger, TypePad...). TOYs who are savvy about attracting readers have been quite successful launching message blogs on their own, as in the examples on the following pages.

GReaT exaPLe OF a "message" BLOG on a PUBLIC/news SITe

Nancy Flanagan: *Stranger in a Strange Land*
http://blogs.edweek.org/teachers/teacher_in_a_strange_land/

Written by 1993 Michigan Teacher of the Year and 30-year veteran K-12 music teacher, Nancy Flanagan, this blog offers Nancy's sharp-eyed perspectives on the inconsistencies and inspirations, the incomprehensible, immoral and imaginative, in American education.

While reading, I often find myself laughing out loud, clenching my jaw, or thinking, "Jeez, she says it so much better than I ever could." Often, I find myself back at work the next day, seeing firsthand *exactly what she was talking about.*

TWO successFUL, seLF-LaUncHeD, message/PLaTFORM BLOGS

Bill Ferriter: *The Tempered Radical*
http://teacherleaders.typepad.com/the_tempered_radical/

(continued on next page)

TWO SUCCESSFUL, SELF-LAUNCHED, MESSAGE/PLATFORM BLOGS *(continued)*

Written by Bill Ferriter, a Regional Teacher of the Year for North Carolina, The Tempered Radical has earned broad recognition for its irreverent takes on topics ranging from the role of media specialists in the public schoolhouse to the damage done to today's students by standardized testing programs.

With a commitment to sharing what he knows about 21st Century Learning and a determination to bridge the gap between policymakers and classroom teachers, Ferriter's work is at once practical and entertaining.

Heather Wolpert-Gawron: *Tween Teacher*
http://tweenteacher.com/

By day, she's a 7th & 8th grade language arts/speech and debate teacher (and a Regional Teacher of the Year for California), but at night, Heather Wolpert-Gawron becomes "Tweenteacher," blogging the latest news in educational policy, curriculum design, and more importantly, how to more deeply enjoy this crazy and difficult calling of ours. She is always pushing us to continue to develop, or reignite, our love for teaching, with all of its obstacles and insults, and ultimately focus on developing our students' love of learning.

Tweenteacher is meant to help new educators, veterans, and second-career teachers navigate through this difficult yet rewarding career. It is also meant to challenge the past practices in our schools that do not work, while highlighting those that do.

CREATING AN IMAGE

The web is really where people create their image these days, and it's the place you're most likely to create your image as a TOY. I had lunch with an entrepreneur recently who told me, "You are who Google says you are." I must admit, I think he has a point. These days, when someone wants to know about you, they type your name into Google. Whatever comes up on that first page is the impression they get.

That said, there are several things you can do to have some control over your image online. We've talked about blogs already, so if you are blogging, those posts are likely to appear. We've also talked about getting media coverage, so if you've been featured in the news, those photos and videos are also forerunners for your first page of Google.

There are two other online locales I'd like to touch on as well:

1) Your Website

If you would like to leverage your TOY award to make a larger difference in education, or to move your career in a certain direction, consider getting your own website. This is where you have the ultimate control over the image you want to present of yourself. You choose the words and images you want to put out to the world about who you are and what work you are doing.

I highly recommend getting a professional to design your site, if you're not a pro at it yourself. But if you have them design it on a platform like WordPress, you can very easily make changes and updates yourself after the design is in place. Adding video gets you ranked higher in Google searches, as does learning about SEO (search engine optimization) — basically keywords you embed into your site for when people search on those topics.

Here are a few examples of TOY websites to check out,

including my own (which is in its second version, the first of which was not nearly as polished!):

✓ http://www.alexkajitani.com

✓ http://www.cindirigsbee.com

✓ http://www.alanlawrencesitomer.com

✓ http://www.philipbigler.com

Check them out and imagine what image you might like to portray of yourself and your work on a website.

2) Your Social Media Presence

So, there's your professional persona on social media — such as setting up a Facebook fan page or a professional Twitter handle and posting about your speeches, articles and what have you. And there's your personal social media presence — where you chat with old high school and college classmates, post your personal photos, etc.

The thing is, when people search for you, they can likely find both (creepy, I know, but it's true). So, as a TOY, you need to think about anything you post on social media as fair game for anyone to find (the definition of "private" has clearly been morphed by social media!) and, thus, part of your image.

This means, of course, photos of you that you would not want seen by your speech audiences, need to not be on social media. It also means the opinions you post can be found, as can the way in which you write or speak. So, take a while to think about your image on social media, any time you post, and what you want to put out to the world — because whatever privacy settings you may have in place, you have to assume they are not failsafe.

OUR social media image

On a broader note, as educators, the image we want to portray of our profession also comes across in what we post in social media.

I've written before about when a colleague of mine posted on Facebook: "Slept 'til noon, hanging at the beach. I love being a teacher on spring break." What message does this send to our non-teacher friends and acquaintances? One of the biggest misperceptions of the teaching profession is that we get "summers off, vacations throughout the year, and only work 6-hour days." This kind of post confirms those inaccurate stereotypes.

We can do a lot to counter stereotypes in the small ways we portray ourselves as teachers on social media. I ask you to really consider how you portray the teaching profession in your posts — and consider showing how hard teachers work, how much we interact with students, how much effort and creativity we put into lesson planning. How about instead of the above post, we post stuff like: "Had an INCREDIBLE discussion with my class today about ways we can use math to be great athletes."

With social media as the dominant form of communication for many of us these days, why not use it to proactively defend the profession we all love so much — and now officially represent as TOYs?

I look forward to the day when I see a commercial for the teaching profession during the SuperBowl, or the day when teachers stand alongside movie stars and professional athletes as some of our country's most visible personalities. However, until then, it is up to us to spread the word about the incredibly challenging, incredibly rewarding work we do. And that is a concept worth "liking."

CHAPTER 12

GETTING PAID:
ENDORSEMENTS, FREE STUFF & BEING A PROFESSIONAL

As teachers, we work in a profession where the traditional expectation is to "give it all away for free." We often arrive at work before our scheduled time, work through recess and lunch, and we stay late. Summers off? Yeah, right…

This may be how it is for us teachers, but it's not how it has to be. When lawyers work for free, they write it off as "pro bono." The main difference between an amateur and a professional is that *professionals get paid*. As teachers, we are professionals. I truly believe that if we are going shift public perceptions to viewing us as the true professionals that we are, then we need to advocate that our time is worth money.

WORK FOR FREE OR FEE?

As a Teacher of the Year, you'll be asked to speak to groups, serve on committees, write articles and more. Most of it will require you to use time aside from your regular teaching duties. Please hear this: *There is nothing greedy or unethical about asking to be compensated for your time.* In fact, I think it's important for us to get comfortable asking to be paid as professionals for our time — and for others to get comfortable paying teachers as professionals for their time outside of the classroom.

Don't get me wrong — I still speak for free on many occasions; however, when I do, the reason usually falls under one of the following three categories:

1) It's a cause/organization I believe in, and they would probably pay me if they could. In other words, *I want to do it*, regardless of pay (and I might even get a free dinner out of it).

2) There will be people in the audience who truly need to hear my message, and can help me support/further my cause. There might also be people in the audience who can hire me to come speak to their group/school.

3) I'm trying out "new material" that I'm not totally comfortable with yet, and I need to try it out before I ask to be paid for it.

HOW TO ASK TO BE COMPENSATED

Of course, asking to be paid for your time is a sticky, often intimidating conversation, and you don't want to look like you're "cashing in" on your new TOY title. Consider using one of the following three responses (feel free to tweak them to fit your needs) when someone asks you to do some work that is outside of your regular day:

1) "This sounds exciting. I need to look at my schedule and prioritize. Can you tell me if there's an honorarium associated with my participating?"

2) "I'd really like to, but I'll need to take time off from work. Would it be possible to cover my travel expenses and include a speaking/working stipend?"

EXPERT ADVICE...

YOU'RE WORTH BEING PAID

"Teachers are kind-hearted by nature. They are in education to teach, not earn millions. That said, there is no reason whatsoever why you, one of the most important members of society, should share your expertise without compensation.

Plenty of people have tried to get me to speak for free or at a very low rate. They scream 'poverty,' yet they have budgets for professional development. I know educational speakers that complain that schools do not pay well. I correct them: 'No, schools do not pay YOU well.'

For those customers who have told me that they could get other speakers for much less than my fees, I assure them that a Volkswagen can get them across the country the same way a Mercedes can: the difference is in the experience.

I have delivered over 1,000 paid speaking engagements internationally, and I can tell you that audiences value you in direct proportion to your compensation. Deliver a free talk, and your audience will think less of your talk. It sounds counter-intuitive, but audiences place greater value on you when they have to PAY you.

Think of wine: which one do guests tend to prefer, the expensive bottle or the Two-Buck Chuck? Advertise yourself as a fine bottle of wine, and you will be treated as such. And I can assure you that your audience will embrace the experience and relish it more."

Danny Brassell, Ph.D.,
"America's Leading Reading Ambassador"
Former classroom teacher, current professor of education,
and successful professional public speaker

3) (You have to be pretty bold to use this one.) "I truly believe that teachers are professionals, and should be compensated for their time, and I need to live by this. Does your budget provide for this?"

If you use any of the above, and the answer is still "No," then laugh it off, and say, "OK, I always make it a point to ask." And then simply decide if you'll still do the work or not.

Whatever you decide, please make sure that being a Teacher of the Year is does not end up costing you a small fortune. To avoid this being "the most expensive award you'll ever receive," be sure to keep track of mileage and other expenses, and speak with your accountant about writing it off.

FRee STUFF

As a Teacher of the Year, you're also going to get free stuff. From hats and pins to cars and computers (yes, one of my colleagues from another state was actually given a BMW to drive for the year), free stuff is often nice (and usually welcomed when given to us teachers). However, sometimes it can also be a bit fraught.

You may not want it, not be able to use it, or feel guilty or self-conscious about it. If it's a guilt thing, I encourage you to stop and consider whether your guilt is warranted, or just an energy-wasting remnant of that old "teachers should give it all away for free — and expect nothing" mentality. (Hint: most, if not all, guilt is energy-wasting!)

That said, there are generally four decisions you can make when given free stuff:

1) Keep it. You deserve it.

2) Give it to your students. If you only have a limited amount,

consider holding a classroom raffle, or give it away as a prize.

3) Give it to another teacher to thank them for their support.

4) Give it to your own children.

FRee money?

Free stuff is nice, but when the "free stuff" is money, things can really start to get sticky.

(I will say here that "free money" is not really an accurate term — I would argue that teachers who are successful at educating their students have earned more than the salary we tend to get, and thus when we are compensated beyond that salary as teacher-leaders, it's basically a "bonus," like most of our corporate colleagues get each year, on top of higher salaries!) Anyway, as we know, the money stuff can get a little touchy in the teacher world.

aLex's STORY

SHOW *WHO* THe money??

Once, while sitting in a staff meeting, our vice principal made a "special announcement." She excitedly told the staff that she had just gotten off the phone with someone from an organization who wanted to celebrate my Teacher of the Year

(continued on next page)

aLeX'S STORY *(continued)*

accomplishment by coming to the school and presenting me with a check for $1,000 at our next staff meeting.

I could instantly feel my colleagues' eyes rolling, and the collective groan. And rightfully so. Here I had spent the month having reporters in my room, being interviewed on the news, and getting quite a bit of attention. And now my colleagues had to watch me get $1,000? I couldn't blame them for being a bit perturbed — especially since we were all working equally as hard (some working much harder than me) to educate our students.

To avoid the awkward situation of having the staff watch me receive a check while they struggled to pay their rent for the month, I immediately went and called the person who would be coming, and suggested that instead of coming to our next staff meeting, that he come and visit my classroom, and meet some of my students as well.

Instead of the situation being one that made people roll their eyes, it turned into an incredible experience for my second period class; they enjoyed having the visitor, and I even had the gentleman talk about his job, along with a short Q&A session with my students!

If you are given money by an organization when you are awarded Teacher of the Year, I encourage you to graciously accept it, and also to be discrete about it among your teaching colleagues. See the chapter on Colleague Relationships for more on this point, but the main point on the "free money" is to keep it in perspective and to keep in mind the sensitivity around money for teachers — among the hardest-working and lowest-paid white-collar professions in our country.

alex's STORY

DEALING WITH DIFFERENCES IN TOY REWARDS

When I (along with four other fabulous educators) was named a San Diego County Teacher of the Year, we were presented with a check for $1,000 and a new laptop at a board meeting. A few months later, I learned that the Orange County Teachers of the Year (just half an hour north of us) were each given $15,000!

I will admit, my initial reaction was that of jealousy. But then I realized something — I was in no position to complain. As long as the Teacher of the Year awards exist, there will be different interpretations of how they should be recognized and rewarded. I decided to be happy for a fellow teacher who had received an award amount usually reserved for other professions.

The truth is, receiving money and gifts is nice. But money gets spent, gifts fall apart, and beauty fades. However, as a Teacher of the Year, the opportunity to create and share ideas is priceless. Stay focused on that.

GIVING TESTIMONIALS

The term "Teacher of the Year" is very powerful. It gives you credibility, authority and prestige. It gives you the right to make decisions as to what is right, what is good, and what is necessary for the betterment of education. People, both inside and outside of education, believe this.

Because they believe this, they will ask you to endorse their products, services and causes. Endorsements and testimonials are a natural part of marketing, and they happen in the business world all the time. Some of the requests I have gotten include:

- Educational materials, such as books, workbooks and software

- Testimonials for websites, or start-up projects

- Drinking water (yes, drinking water)

- Political candidates and ballot propositions

- Letters of recommendations for colleagues (*tons* — who wouldn't want a letter of recommendation from a Teacher of the Year?)

Some TOY-selecting organizations have strict guidelines on what you can and cannot endorse, so be sure you know the "rules" of your particular award. For many of us, though, it's up to us how we want to handle these requests. If this is the case for you, be sure to think about both the positive and negative effects that endorsing something or someone can have. At first, I wanted to help as many people as I could, so I usually said "yes" to most requests.

While they all seemed like small favors and small decisions, I began to realize that endorsing a book might actually convince someone to purchase that book. Writing a letter of recommendation might make the difference in who gets a coveted job. If the book is wonderful and can help a lot of people, it's a pleasure to see other people reading it on my recommendation. It's also very powerful when a fantastic colleague calls to say, "I got the job!" and to thank you for your support.

Of course, if the the book is a dud, or the person is someone that we just didn't want to say "no" to, that ultimately reflects badly on us as individuals and as Teachers of the Year. And, it doesn't even necessarily create what we are looking to create for education!

Over the years, I've gotten much better at knowing what to say "yes" and "no" to, when it comes to putting my name as an endorsement on someone else's program, product or job application. And I've created some "guidelines" for myself that also help me decide what to agree to. For example, I decided that when it comes to politics, I am not comfortable endorsing an individual candidate, but I am comfortable endorsing a ballot proposition that supports education.

You will find your own comfort zone when it comes to endorsements — and don't worry, you are likely to make a few missteps on your way to finding it. Always come back to who you are as a teacher and a person, and stick to your own values (and your own platform, as we discuss in the Platform chapter). Like many other types of influence, "Teacher of the Year" influence is strong and powerful. Use it wisely!

TOY TALK ...

"Being selected as a Teacher of the Year is a tremendous honor, but it comes with a significant responsibility. The title provides an unparalleled opportunity to share with a diverse audience the power of education to help transform a student's life."

Kelly Kovacic, *California Teacher of the Year*

CHAPTER 13

JUGGLING THE JUGGLE:
TOY-LIFE BALANCE & SELF CARE

One of the most memorable experiences I had as the 2009 California Teacher of the Year was getting the opportunity (along with every state's Teacher of the Year) to visit the White House, on President Barack Obama's 99th day in office. It was President Obama's first-ever ceremony in the Rose Garden, the weather was absolutely beautiful, and somehow, I was fortunate enough to be standing right next to the First Couple during this group shot. But here's what this photo doesn't show:

- The day this photo was taken, I had gained 20 pounds since being named California Teacher of the Year.

- My pants were so tight that it was causing my lower back to hurt.

- Carpal Tunnel Syndrome had crept into both of my arms — the result of so many late nights working on my computer on all of my new "Teacher of the Year" responsibilities.

- It was the third day of me being gone for eight straight days while my wife stayed in California to care for our newborn son and three-year-old daughter. I had quite a few trips that year where I was gone for several days at a time, and it was stressful for the whole family.

While being a Teacher of the Year is an honor and a gift, it is also a role that can leave you unhealthy and unhappy, if you're not careful. I can't tell you how many fancy dinners I attended, only to return to my hotel room having overeaten and feeling sick. In addition, I felt insanely guilty for not being at home to help my wife with our newborn son and toddler daughter. Take the time to ensure that this award does not come at the cost of your physical and mental health, or at the expense of your family.

Balance and self-care can be hard to maintain on a regular teacher's schedule, but when you add TOY responsibilities to the mix, it becomes *absolutely* critical to find ways to care for yourself and your relationships. Here's another area where connecting with other TOYs can help you validate your feelings and discuss strategies during the intensity of your TOY year and beyond. It also helps to make a commitment to yourself to pay attention to signs of stress, and shift whatever you can when those signs start flashing red.

TOY TALK ...

"In all things, seek to maintain balance. A balance between expert and beginner, a balance between assertiveness and humility, and a especially a balance between the demands of this new position and your family.

There have been too many Teachers of the Year who have responded to this great honor with zeal and fervor, but neglected to take care of themselves and their own relationships. It's demanding, it's time consuming, it's a new world that you have entered. Be sure to bring those that you love along on the journey with you.

And take time to step away from the journey altogether to do the things you love to do with the people you love the most. It's okay to say no when people ask you to make one more speech, serve on one more panel, or chaperone one more dance. Be honest with them and tell them that you're overextended right now, but that you'd be happy to suggest some other experts to act as your stunt double.

So enjoy this crazy ride, but don't enjoy it alone. Find balance."

Michael Geisen, *National Teacher of the Year*

EXPERT ADVICE...

NURTURE YOURSELF, SERVE OTHERS BETTER

"Self nurturing is essential for living mindfully, open heartedly and with less stress. This is especially true when living a public life, like when you're Teacher of the Year. Although you may wonder how you will find time to care for yourself while fulfilling so many new commitments, I believe it is critical to establish a regular self care practice for your experience to be rich, fulfilling and meaningful.

Self nurturing *need not be time consuming*, it just requires you to identify what deeply nourishes you, helps you value yourself and encourages your own potential and growth. My top five ways to start self nurturing include:

1) Begin a gratitude practice — write down 5 things you are grateful for every day,

2) Create a list of activities that bring you joy — commit to trying a different activity daily,

3) Take a walk in nature or spend even just a few minutes outside appreciating the sights, sounds and beauty,

4) Connect with your breath, a few times a day, pause and focus on your breath, moving in and out, and connect with the present moment,

5) Set an intention (like peace, joy, compassion, forgiveness, love, trust, courage, creativity, etc.) for your day, and reflect on how it manifests and what insights and wisdom you learn about yourself.

(continued on next page)

> ## EXPERT ADVICE *(continued)*...
>
> Commit to nurturing yourself throughout this process and you will find the true gift is living authentically while sharing with the world what you love. Your experience will be enriched as a result, and your ability to be truly present in this process will benefit not only you, but everyone in your life.
>
> Prioritize self nurturing and make this Teacher of the Year experience one of the best of your life!"
>
> **Kelley Grimes, M.S.W.,** *Counselor, Mentor and Artist, specializing in Self Nurturing Tools*

So, I'm now back to my normal weight and energy level, after doing a major green juice cleanse with my wife (we do live in Southern California, after all!), shifting my eating, and getting back to a more regular exercise routine after the dust settled from the most intense period of my TOY work. In hindsight, the lack of balance in my TOY year offered me some valuable lessons about self-care that I take with me through today. I'd love to help other TOYs maintain more balance during their year in the spotlight and beyond.

That said, I offer one more tip as well: plan a *real break — at least* 10 days — where you are *not working*, as soon as your TOY school year lets out. You will have been working extra hard, on all levels, this school year, and knowing you will have that time to regroup and reconnect can help you through the hardest days (and help your relationships recover from the year, too — more on that next!).

> ## TOY TALK ...
>
> "Take care of yourself! If you currently work out, don't stop, no matter how busy you get. If you don't work out, start. I got great at writing and practicing speeches on the treadmill!"
>
> **Derek Olson,** *Minnesota Teacher of the Year*

COMING HOME

It would be incomplete to talk about the Teacher of the Year experience without discussing the effects of the TOY spotlight on our spouses/partners. Our spouses and partners are the ones who see us undergo the Teacher of the Year process from beginning to end, and who continue to offer support as we grow and evolve as teacher-leaders.

It's important to remember that our life being changed by the TOY award is also *their* life being changed by the TOY award. And if you have kids, this means their lives', too — and that the responsibilities for the kids usually fall more onto your spouse than ever during your TOY year, so double whammy! For the best perspective on TOY partner relationships, I thought it was most fitting to hear from the spouses themselves.

First, here's a spouse story from my own wife (and writing partner), Megan Pincus Kajitani, who has some insights about the emotions of a spouse "left behind," at home with small children, during my TOY activities:

MEGAN KAJITANI'S STORY

AND THAT'S OK!

When Alex was selected as San Diego County TOY, I was newly pregnant with our second child, and we had a toddler. When he was selected as California TOY, I was quite pregnant. And, when he was selected as a Top-4 Finalist for National TOY — which meant that he was invited on two out-of-state trips to compete for the top honor — I was about to burst. In fact, Alex had to miss the first trip, to Texas, because I was giving birth!

I still remember him on a conference call with people at the Texas conference as I lay in bed with our just-born baby. Then, a few weeks later, he was off to Washington, D.C., to hang out with the newly-elected President and Vice President (and go through some intense interviews). My brother, who lives in Maryland, got to use my ticket to go the White House event with Alex, while I was home, overwhelmingly postpartum, with equally overwhelmed toddler, and a new baby nursing day and night.

Alex talks about the guilt he felt, and the mixed feelings he had, about going off on TOY stuff while I was chained to home. Ironically — and what I think is important for both partners to understand — I had the *exact same mixed feelings and guilt!* I wanted him to go have these amazing experiences, make a difference, establish himself. And, I wanted him home with us. I was thrilled about all the attention and opportunities he was getting. And, I was also sad and frustrated that I didn't get to go along for the ride, or have those kinds of experiences of my own.

(continued on next page)

MEGAN KAJITANI'S STORY *(continued)*

I even taught our daughter, who was three when her little brother was born and her daddy traveled the country as California TOY, about the term "mixed feelings." It helped her to process both her feelings about having a new sibling, as well as about her daddy and mommy not being as available as they used to be. "It's when you feel happy and sad about something, all at the same time — and that's OK!" she still says.

Looking back, given our circumstances, I'm not really sure what we could've done to make it less intense for our family. Perhaps just knowing going in to expect these kinds of mixed feelings — and being OK with them, in both of us — would've eased our tension a bit.

So, I offer this to any TOY couples (because it is a joint effort!) — especially those with young children: honor your own, and your partner's, mixed feelings about the changes the award can bring to your lifestyle for a time. Don't take those feelings personally, or resent them in your partner. Remember that you're in it together, that the intensity of the year will pass, and that, if you allow it to, the TOY award can move your life in new directions that will better serve your whole family in the long run.

And now we have the story of Manny Aceves, whose wife, Andee, was a California Teacher of the Year the year before me. Manny is a teacher himself, and has great insights to share about being a TOY spouse without kids in the house (in other words, literally coming along for the ride!):

manny aceves' STORY

THE CARE AND FEEDING OF A TOY

I remember coming home from church one Sunday morning to hear a voice message from the state superintendent of education informing us that my wife, Andee, had been selected as one of the 2008 California Teachers of the Year. I remember my surprise as if it was yesterday (my wife never did erase the message!). While full of excitement, joy, and pride, at the same time I also realized that our lives were going to change dramatically. I knew my wife was going to need my help to survive and thrive during the next year.

So, here are some lessons I've learned over the years to share with spouses/significant others of TOYs. You see, behind every successful TOY, there is someone else doing the laundry.

1) **Be willing to juggle home responsibilities.**

 Being empty nesters, one of the things I agreed to be responsible for was the daily cooking. This relieved a lot of stress in our home because that year my wife often came home from work hours after I did from my school day. So while Andee was correcting papers, planning for the next day, and responding to countless emails, I prepared dinner for us. It worked out well for the both of us.

 (continued on next page)

manny aceves' STORY *(continued)*

2) **Be willing to juggle home responsibilities, Part 2.**

Periodically revisiting home responsibilities became apparent two years later when Andee beat me home one day, and was sitting on the sofa, catching up on schoolwork. Opening up the door, after my long day of teaching and school meetings, I was greeted with, "Honey, Thank God you're home! I'm starving!" The look on my wife's face showed me she instantly knew she had put her foot in her mouth. And while I did prepare the dinner that night (I had stopped by the store to prepare something special), we agreed that — now that her reigning TOY year was over — whenever either one of us beat the other home, it would be their responsibility to start dinner.

3) **Know when to support and when to suggest solutions.**

This has taken me years of learning. I finally realized that most times when my wife was feeling overwhelmed with the daily grind of TOY responsibilities, all she really wanted was a shoulder to cry on and someone to hear her out. Too often, I went straight to a man's superhero strength of "problem solving." This was often the last thing she wanted to hear. There is a time and a place for that, but it never is the first thing you should do.

(continued on next page)

manny aceves' STORY *(continued)*

4) **Become knowledgeable of good wine and massage techniques.**

   Trust me on this. Wine and a massage are a surefire way to relieve the stress of a TOY. There is nothing that can't be relieved by a glass of wine and foot massage. However, be sure to implement the glass of wine and foot massage only after work is over for the night. This powerful combo will achieve total relaxation and take away any motivation to continue working. Use with caution!

5) **Enjoy being an escort for the many social functions you'll attend, whether you're a teacher or not.**

   There will be many evening functions you will be expected to attend. The good news is that the people attending are some of the most interesting and amiable people you'll ever meet. Mingling is not a difficult task. I have often left an event re-energized about education because of the conversations I had with these great teachers. Not only that, you'll earn a bunch of Brownie points from your spouse as well.

   And one more tip, just for TOY partners who are also teachers themselves:

6) **For Teacher-Partners: Beware of "TOY-in-Training" Syndrome.**

(continued on next page)

manny aceves' STORY *(continued)*

Only spouses or significant others of TOYs who are also teachers need to read further. OK, don't be surprised if you experience the following scenario at one of the social functions you'll attend. When mingling, eventually you share that you are a teacher as well. For some reason, some people feel obligated to say something like, "Don't worry, I'm sure that you'll become a Teacher of the Year soon. You too must be a great teacher." I've experienced this more than once, so I created the title TOY-in-Training, and I enjoyed using it.

I know they mean well, but not all great teachers become TOYs. TOYs are really spokespersons for all the great teachers they represent. I know many amazing teachers who prefer to be low-key and not get in the limelight that is required of TOYs. I usually tried to laugh it off and counter with some humorous comment.

The care and feeding of a TOY is a serious undertaking, and not for the feint of heart. I've had a great experience and you will, too. My final words of encouragement are to enjoy your TOY's 15 minutes of fame knowing that there's no way in &%#* they would have ever made it without your support!

Just as you remember who you are as a teacher to stay balanced as a TOY, it's also so important to remember who you are *as a person* — and of course your significant other is a big piece of who you are. If you approach the year as a team, it's all the easier to reap the benefits of this amazing experience as a team as well.

CARING FOR "THE KIDS" (I.E., YOUR STUDENTS) DURING YOUR TOY YEAR

One more issue of balance "on the homefront" comes up with every TOY I know — that of managing your classroom during your TOY year while you are often away. In fact, for State Teachers of the Year Deborah Fogg (New Hampshire), Deb Wickerman (Ohio), and Margaret Williams (Missouri), managing your classroom well while you're away on TOY duties was the top piece of advice they wanted to offer new TOYs!

Here are their — and my — combined strategies to care for your students while you're off on TOY duties:

1) **Find one great sub who can commit to covering all of the days you are out.**

    Says Margaret Williams, Missouri TOY: "The new TOY should have a conversation shortly after their selection with their principal or superintendent about obtaining one substitute teacher who will always substitute for the new TOY when they were not available to be in their classroom for STOY business *and anything else.* The best substitute teacher would be a person who is recently retired from the new TOY's school, who taught in the school, taught the same subject or grade level of the new TOY, can substitute any time during the school year, and *most of all* be a great teacher (or have as many of these qualities as possible).

    Time should be *planned* for the two teachers to talk and become familiar with the expectations and procedures of the new TOY. The substitute teacher should be allowed to have *at least one paid day* when all they do is observe all of the classes and lessons of the new TOY to "experience" the expectations and procedures discussed. Of course all kinds of contact information should be exchanged and they should have a 'plan b' just in case an emergency comes up when neither of them is available."

2) Don't stress about being out of class.

Says Deborah Fogg, New Hampshire TOY: "As hard as it is to imagine, the school day will go on without you. I had a really hard time letting go of the idea that I am the only one who can be in my room. Lastly, I want you to enjoy all the activities that are part of your TOY experience. It comes once in a lifetime!"

I think I wasted too much time feeling guilty about being out of my classroom (again, guilt: usually an energy-wasting emotion!). While it may not have been my best teaching year, content-wise, my students all told me at the end of the year how exciting and inspiring it was for them to be a part of my journey (well, in middle schoolers' words, but that was the gist) — having camera crews in class, seeing me with President Obama, and getting a taste of what doing one's job well can bring. As we know well, sometimes teaching is about more than just academic content.

3) Make the most of the time you are in class.

Says Deb Wickerman, Ohio TOY: "Love your time with your students, treasure it. … Even though this is a time of testing, testing, testing, don't forget to utilize any teachable moment that comes along."

This can be challenging, but it's important: when you're there with your students, try to really *be there* with them. (Advice that applies to your family, too.) Pay attention to them, and try to quickly home in on what they need from you when you're there. You will have less days with them, so make the most of those days by upping your teaching game each day you are in class. (Remember, you are going to plan a real break for when the school year ends!)

TOY TALK ...

"The mediocre teacher tells. The good teacher explains. The superior teacher demonstrates. The great teacher inspires."

— *William Arthur Ward*

How does a great teacher inspire? In my years of working with the Wisconsin Teachers of the Year, I can truly say that these teachers continue to find the "joy of teaching" no matter what!

No matter that school safety is concerning, no matter that such large numbers of students require individual learning plans, no matter that more and more of our children live in poverty, no matter what... these inspiring educators will always bring joy to their classrooms through their joy of teaching. Thank goodness!"

Elaine Strom, *Teacher of the Year Coordinator,*
Wisconsin Department of Public Instruction

In short, juggling the juggle as a TOY may not always be easy, but you can be successful with some good strategies in your pocket and support in your corner. Above all, be gentle on yourself and your loved ones, and simply do your best to juggle being a teacher, a TOY, and just *you*. One day at a time!

CHAPTER 14

AFTER "YOUR YEAR":
STAYING RELEVANT

{
"Today's newspaper is tomorrow's
fish and chips wrapper."

— Unknown
}

There is no such thing as a former Teacher of the Year. You may not be the current, reigning TOY for your state, district, county, or organization, but you will ALWAYS be a Teacher of the Year, and one of the best things you can do is get comfortable with your title. It's been few years since I was named the 2009 California Teacher of the Year, but I am still identified as "California Teacher of the Year" all the time. I've found that people don't really care what year it was, they only care that you are.

For many, it's a complete relief when your official term ends, and you get to hand the title over to the next person(s). However, it is important to remember that being named a TOY is not only an award in recognition for a job well done; rather, *it is an expectation for future behavior.* If we completely drop out of the mix after our TOY year and become "tomorrow's fish and chips wrapper," have we truly lived up to all that we were selected to do — which includes continuing to improve education both in and beyond our classrooms?

Staying relevant does not have to mean staying in the spotlight. But, to use your award to create positive change, affect lives, and pursue your passion is to capitalize on the award in its highest form. Some go on to start or run their own schools, others take leadership roles in their school, district or community, some branch out on their own to work for education in their way, and some return to the same classroom they've been teaching in for many years. All options are worthwhile and wonderful.

TOY TALK ...

"My words of advice are to never allow the title, Teacher of the Year, to suggest we rest on our laurels. It might be tempting to believe our work is done and the pinnacle has been reached. Instead, let's consider the honor as a challenge to work even harder and more purposefully so that we can take advantage of the platform we have received.

We have an amazing opportunity to strengthen our profession and rekindle passion amongst our peers, so let's continue to do the good work we have begun!"

Andee Aceves, *California Teacher of the Year*

TIPS FOR STAYING IN THE MIX

Regardless of your pursuit, here are three things you can do to stay relevant and engaged as a Teacher of the Year:

1) **Continue networking.** Send cards, emails, articles, etc. and keep your TOY title on your business cards, in your email signature, and anywhere else you feel necessary. Many TOYs (myself included) have found these more passive ways to keep our title in play may be more

comfortable than saying it aloud when we introduce ourselves. The power of the title may actually come *after* a great conversation with someone, when they look down at your business card after you've parted ways and discover that they've been talking to a Teacher of the Year.

If you have ideas for projects, pursue them! Your TOY title can continue to open doors for you. Want to write a book, start a non-profit, sit on a policy committee? Keep voicing these goals as you talk to people, and it's amazing what can manifest. If someone is doing work in education that inspires you, reach out to them! Drop them a line. Offer to collaborate or contribute. Your opportunities are limitless, it's just a matter of how much energy you put into connecting with others who can help you pursue your goals.

2) **Keep in touch with other Teachers of the Year that you meet.** The work that they are doing will keep you inspired over the years. Support them in their pursuits and projects, and let them know what you're up to. Consider teaming up with them on projects.

When a Teacher of the Year does something — that's significant. However, when a group of Teachers of the Year does something — that can be truly *transformative*.

3) **Think of your character as defined by the headlines.** Being aware of your "Teacher of the Year" title can often serve as a moral compass when faced with some of life's tough decisions (even when they're quick judgement calls). When faced with any decision that may border on ethical/ unethical or good/poor judgement, picture the story about you appearing the next day in a newspaper, where the headline reads "Teacher of the Year (fill in the blank with "gets DUI, is arrested, etc.")." Too many times, I've seen the headlines reflect poorly on a TOY, which thus reflects poorly on all teachers and our entire profession.

Remember: if a teacher drives drunk, it's bad; if a Teacher of the Year drives drunk, it's a major headline. I'm not saying you're going to drive drunk, shoplift or have an inappropriate sexual relationship. I use this moral compass for my typically mundane ethical decisions, like returning the car seat Babies-R-Us mistakenly didn't charge me a penny for. (Imagine: "Teacher of the Year Steals $200 Car Seat!") And you should have seen the woman's face when I returned it!

I played this mind game with myself before I was a TOY as well, in the context of being a teacher; but the stakes go up when we become TOYs, giving us more to gain and more to lose. In short, considering the award you've received in advance of taking an action can help you remain in good reputation — a key to staying relevant! — long after your "official" term has ended.

TOY TALK ...

"If there's anything I've learned in working with Teachers of the Year for over 20 years it is to remember who you are — A TEACHER! That is why you were selected for the role. That is what you know inside and out.

Any situation you find yourself in and are unsure of what to do, put it in a teacher/student context and you'll know what your direction needs to be. TEACH. That's what you do."

Jon Quam, *Director,*
National Teacher of the Year Program

ALWAYS A TEACHER, ALWAYS A TOY

As your year in the spotlight as a TOY comes to an end, in many ways it is just the beginning. I've said several times in this book, and I truly mean it, your experience as a TOY is invaluable, and comes with limitless, long-term potential.

I hope this book helps you navigate your Teacher of the Year experience, and provides some strategies and support for you as you step into this new phase of your career as a teacher-leader. I'm truly honored to walk among, get to know, and work with fellow TOYs every day. I find that what we have in common — our motivation and inspiration as teachers — ties us together in ways that go beyond a title, but to the core of who we are.

Thank you for reading, and I hope to connect with you further online or in person. I truly believe that, working together, we can elevate education and our profession in this country — as teacher-leaders who are poised to make a difference.

TOY TALK ...

"The confirmation and affirmation this honor will bring will stay with you always. I hope that this insight will take some of the pressure off of the year you serve.

The impact you want to have, the things you want to accomplish, do not have to happen before your term is up; they may take years to unfold.

Being Teacher of the Year will change you, permanently, in ways that make meeting those goals so much more possible."

Diana Leddy, *Vermont Teacher of the Year*

WE'D LOVE TO HEAR FROM YOU!

Please continue the conversation with us by "liking" and commenting on our Facebook page (search "Teacher of the Year Handbook") or email us at AlexKajitani@gmail.com. We look forward to connecting with you!

ABOUT THE AUTHORS:

Alex Kajitani and Megan Pincus Kajitani are the co-founders of Kajitani Education, which provides teacher education and lifestyle education, with the motto: *"educating for the world as it can be."* Together, Alex and Megan create books, trainings and online programs to inform and connect those who aspire to create a better world.

Alex Kajitani Alex Kajitani is the 2009 California Teacher of the Year and a Top-Four Finalist for National Teacher of the Year. He is the author of the acclaimed book, *Owning It: Proven Strategies for Success in ALL of Your Roles as a Teacher Today*, and is a leading authority on teacher leadership.

Alex delivers powerful keynote speeches and workshops across the United States to support and motivate teachers. His TED Talk hit over 10,000 views in 2013, and his work has been praised by education leader Dr. Harry K. Wong *(The First Days of School)* as "some of the most creative work I've ever seen a teacher do."

Also known around the country as "The Rappin' Mathematician," Alex's CDs and Activity Books are being used in homes and classrooms around the world, and he writes a regular column for teachers of at-risk students. He has been featured in many education books and media outlets, including *The CBS Evening News with Katie Couric.*

To learn more about Alex's work, and to invite him to inspire your group, visit www.AlexKajitani.com.

Megan Pincus Kajitani is a professional writer and educator for over 17 years. She has written columns and essays for newspapers, magazines, books and online media outlets, including *The Chronicle of Higher Education, The Huffington Post, Inside Higher Ed, Mothering Magazine,* and others. She has worked as a journalist, editor, college teacher and career counselor, and, most recently, as a conscious lifestyle educator — always combining her passions for writing, teaching and changing the world.

Megan has a Master's degree in Media & Cultural Studies from the University of Wisconsin-Madison, and completed Ph.D. coursework and a Certificate in Training & Career Development at the University of California-San Diego. She also trained in plant-based nutrition and humane education to launch her latest project, Giraffe Revolution. Learn more about Megan and her work at **www.GiraffeRevolution.com**.

23891022R00075

Made in the USA
San Bernardino, CA
03 February 2019